AN
O. HENRY READER

AN ADAPTED CLASSIC

AN
O. HENRY READER

O. HENRY

GLOBE BOOK COMPANY
A Division of Simon & Schuster
Englewood Cliffs, New Jersey

Edited by Lou P. Bunce
former head of the English Department
Highland Park High School
Highland Park, New Jersey

Adapted by Roger B. Goodman
Chairman of the English Department
Stuyvesant High School
New York, New York

Acknowledgments

"The Ransom of Red Chief," copyright 1907 by Doubleday & Company, Inc., "The Third Ingredient,""Schools and Schools," copyright 1908 by Doubleday & Company, Inc., "Rus in Urbe," copyright 1909 by Doubleday & Company, Inc., "The Gift of the Magi," "The Skylight Room," "The Cop and the Anthem," "Mammon and the Archer," "Springtime A La Carte," "The Romance of a Busy Broker," "After Twenty Years,""The Furnished Room," "A Retrieved Reformation," "The Whirligig of Life," "The Clarion Call," "A Lickpenny Lover," "One Thousand Dollars," "While the Auto Waits," "The Last Leaf," "Girl" all from the book THE COMPLETE WORKS OF O. HENRY. Reprinted by permission of Doubleday & Company, Inc.

Illustrations by Joe Forte, Larry Johnson, Karen Kretschmann, Michael Tedesco, Lynda West

Cover design: Marek Antoniak
Cover illustration: Angelo Franco

ISBN:0-83590-269-2

Printed in the United States of America.
10   9   8   7   6   5   4

Globe Book Company
A Division of Simon & Schuster
Englewood Cliffs, New Jersey

Adapter's Note

In preparing this edition of AN O. HENRY READER, we have kept the author's main purpose in mind. However, language has changed since the stories were originally published. We have modified or omitted some passages and vocabulary in the stories, but we have kept as much of the original language as possible. In order to assist you with the vocabulary, footnotes have been included in this edition.

While reading these stories you should keep in mind that O. Henry was a famous realist in his writings. He strove to show what the common person felt and thought in the early 1900s. So if you read a passage in a story that views people in a stereotyped way remember the time in which these stories were written. These passages were kept in the stories in order to retain the flavor of O. Henry's writing.

About the Author

O. Henry's life was as full of unexpected twists as any of his stories. He was born William Sidney Porter in 1862 in Greensboro, North Carolina. At the age of 15 he left school to work in a local drugstore. After four years, he moved to Texas, where he lived on a sheep ranch. Two years later he moved to the city of Austin, Texas. In Austin, O. Henry married and held a string of different jobs: druggist, bookkeeper, draftsman, bankteller, and newspaper reporter.

O. Henry lost a job as a bankteller when $1,000 was discovered to be missing from his accounts. Though many people thought O. Henry was innocent, the bank decided to press charges against him. Rather than face trial, O. Henry fled to Honduras. But when O. Henry heard his wife was ill, he returned to Texas. There he was tried, convicted, and sent to prison.

In prison, O. Henry started writing short stories using the pen name "O. Henry." Scholars think that he got this name from Orrin Henry, captain of the guards where O. Henry was imprisoned. After serving three years of a five year sentence, O. Henry was released for good behavior. He moved to New York and supported himself there by writing.

O. Henry's stories were very popular during his lifetime. His life out West and in New York provided him with the raw material for his stories. His experiences had given him sympathy for the underdog—the poor, reformed criminals, and hobos. His stories affectionately describe the lives of shopgirls, typists, clerks, and occasionally the rich. O. Henry's tales are also loved because of their surprise endings—those final twists that catch you off guard. In all, O. Henry wrote over 300 short stories before his death in 1910. He is remembered as one of America's favorite short story writers.

Preface

In these stories you will meet many different characters. You will be introduced to Soapy the hobo, the fierce Red Chief, the reformed criminal Jimmy Valentine, and the loyal farmer Walter. Some of the characters will be very poor, and others will be extremely wealthy. But O. Henry shows us that no matter how much money a person has, we all have the same emotions: love, ambition, and loyalty.

Most of O. Henry's stories take place in New York City during the early 1900s. O. Henry fills his stories with descriptions of boarding houses, department stores, park benches, cheap restaurants, and occasional glimpses into the world of wealth. This world may at first seem very distant to you. But no matter how different things are today, you will recognize the people in O. Henry's stories. That is the reason why O. Henry is still read today—he was true to his time while describing what is constant in human nature.

—H.B.

Contents

The Cop
and the
Anthem

*So you think it's easy to get arrested? Soapy thought so too,
until he tried it one cold fall day.*

On his bench in Madison Square Soapy moved uneasily.
When wild geese honk high of nights, and when women
without sealskin coats grow kind to their husbands, and when
Soapy moves uneasily on his bench in the park, you may
know that winter is near at hand.

A dead leaf fell in Soapy's lap. That was Jack Frost's
card. Jack is kind to the people of Madison Square, and gives
fair warning of his annual call. At the corners of four streets
he hands his card to the North Wind, footman of the mansion
of All Outdoors, so that the inhabitants may make ready.

Soapy's mind became aware of the fact that the time had
come for him to make himself into a singular Committee of
Ways and Means to provide against the coming cold. And
therefore he moved uneasily on his bench.

The ambitions of Soapy were not of the highest. In them
were no considerations of Mediterranean cruises, of Southern
skies or drifting in the Vesuvian Bay. Three months on the
Island[1] was what his soul craved. Three months of assured

---

[1] The Island: Blackwells, now known as Welfare Island in New York
City's East River. Here were once located charitable institutions and
prisons.

board and bed and friendly company, safe from Boreas[2] and bluecoats, seemed desirable to Soapy.

For years the hospitable Blackwells had been his winter quarters. Just as his more fortunate fellow New Yorkers had bought their tickets to Palm Beach and the Riviera each winter, so Soapy had made his humble arrangements for his annual trip to the Island. And now the time was come. On the previous night three newspapers, distributed beneath his coat, about his ankles and over his lap, had failed to repulse the cold as he slept on his bench near the spurting fountain in the ancient square. So the Island loomed big and timely in Soapy's mind. He scorned the provisions made in the name of charity for the city's dependents. In Soapy's opinion the Law was more helpful than Philanthropy. There was an endless round of institutions where he might receive lodging and food accordant with the simple life. But to one of Soapy's proud spirit the gifts of charity are hard to bear. If not in coin you must pay in humiliation of spirit for every benefit received at the hands of philanthropy. Every bed of charity must have its toll of a bath, every loaf of bread its compensation of a private and personal investigation. Wherefore it is better to be a guest of the law, which, though conducted by rules, does not meddle unduly with a gentleman's private affairs.

Soapy, having decided to go to the Island, at once set about accomplishing his desire. There were many easy ways of doing this. The pleasantest was to dine luxuriously at some expensive restaurant; and then, after declaring himself penniless, to be handed over quietly and without uproar to a policeman. An accommodating magistrate would do the rest.

Soapy left his bench and strolled out of the square and across the level sea of asphalt, where Broadway and Fifth Avenue flow together. Up Broadway he turned, and halted at a glittering café, where are gathered together nightly the

---

[2] Boreas: ancient Greek personification of the north wind.

choicest products of the grape, the silkworm, and the protoplasm.

Soapy had confidence in himself from the lowest button of his vest upward. He was shaven, and his coat was decent and his neat black, ready-tied four-in-hand had been presented to him by a lady missionary on Thanksgiving day. If he could reach a table in the restaurant unsuspected success would be his. The portion of him that would show above the table would raise no doubt in the waiter's mind. A roasted mallard duck, thought Soapy, would be about the thing—with a bottle of Chablis, and then Camembert, a demitasse and a cigar. One dollar for the cigar would be enough. The total would not be so high as to call forth any real revenge from the café management; and yet the meat would leave him filled and happy for the journey to his winter refuge.

But as Soapy set foot inside the restaurant door the head waiter's eye fell upon his frayed trousers and worn shoes. Strong and ready hands turned him about and conveyed him in silence and haste to the sidewalk.

Soapy turned off Broadway. It seemed that his route to the coveted Island was not to be an epicurean[3] one. Some other way of entering limbo must be thought of.

At a corner of Sixth Avenue electric lights and cunningly displayed wares behind plate glass made a shop window conspicuous. Soapy took a cobblestone and dashed it through the glass. People came running around the corner, a policeman in the lead. Soapy stood still, with his hands in his pockets, and smiled at the sight of brass buttons.

"Where's the man that done that?" inquired the officer, excitedly.

"Don't you figure out that I might have had something to do with it?" said Soapy, not without sarcasm, but friendly, as one greets good fortune.

The policeman's mind refused to accept Soapy even as a clue. Men who smash windows do not remain to parley with

---

[3] Epicurean: pertaining to one who is fond of luxury.

the law. They take to their heels. The policeman saw a man halfway down the block running to catch a car. With drawn club he joined in the pursuit. Soapy, with disgust in his heart, loafed along, twice unsuccessful.

On the opposite side of the street was a restaurant of no great pretensions. It catered to large appetites and modest purses. Its crockery and atmosphere were thick. Its soup and napery thin. Into this place Soapy took his old, worn shoes and telltale trousers without challenge. At a table he sat and consumed beefsteak, flapjacks, doughnuts, and pie. And then to the waiter he betrayed the fact that the minutest coin and himself were strangers.

"Now, get busy and call a cop," said Soapy. "And don't keep a gentleman waiting."

"No cop for youse," said the waiter, with a voice like butter cakes and an eye like the cherry in a Manhattan cocktail. "Hey, Con!"

Neatly upon his left ear on the callous pavement two waiters pitched Soapy. He arose joint by joint, as a carpenter's rule opens, and beat the dust from his clothes. Arrest seemed but a rosy dream. The Island seemed very far away. A policeman who stood before a drugstore two doors away laughed and walked down the street.

Five blocks Soapy travelled before his courage permitted him to woo capture again. This time the opportunity presented what he termed to himself a "cinch." A young woman of a modest and pleasing guise was standing before a show window gazing with sprightly interest at its display of shaving mugs and inkstands, and two yards from the window a large policeman leaned against a water plug.

It was Soapy's design to assume the role of the despicable "masher." The refined and elegant appearance of his victim and the nearness of the conscientious cop encouraged him to believe that he would soon feel the pleasant official clutch upon his arm that would insure his winter quarters on the right little, tight little isle.

Soapy straightened the lady missionary's ready-made tie,

dragged his shrinking cuffs into the open, set his hat at a killing angle and sidled toward the young woman. He made eyes at her, was taken with sudden coughs and "hems," smiled, smirked, and went brazenly through the impudent and contemptible act of the "masher." With half an eye Soapy saw that the policeman was watching him fixedly. The young woman moved away a few steps and again bestowed her absorbed attention upon the shaving mugs. Soapy followed, boldly stepping to her side, raised his hat and said:

"Ah there, Bedelia! Don't you want to come and play in my yard?"

The policeman was still looking. The persecuted young woman had but to beckon a finger and Soapy would be practically en route for his island haven. Already he imagined he could feel the cozy warmth of the station house. The young woman faced him and, stretching out a hand, caught Soapy's coat sleeve.

"Sure, Mike," she said, joyfully, "if you'll blow me to a pail of suds. I'd have spoke to you sooner, but the cop was watching."

With the young woman playing the clinging ivy to his oak Soapy walked past the policeman overcome with gloom. He seemed doomed to liberty.

At the next corner he shook off his companion and ran. He halted in the district where by night are found the lightest streets, hearts, vows, and songs. Women in furs and men in greatcoats moved gaily in the wintry air. A sudden fear seized Soapy that some dreadful enchantment had rendered him immune to arrest. The thought brought a little of panic upon it, and when he came upon another policeman lounging grandly in front of a transplendent theatre he caught at the immediate straw of "disorderly conduct."

On the sidewalk Soapy began to yell drunken gibberish at the top of his harsh voice. He danced, howled, raved, and otherwise disturbed the peace.

The policeman twirled his club, turned his back to Soapy and remarked to a citizen.

"'Tis one of them Yale lads celebratin' the goose egg they give to the Hartford College. Noisy; but no harm. We've instructions to lave them be."

Disconsolate, Soapy ceased his racket. Would never a policeman lay hands on him? In his fancy the Island seemed an unattainable Arcadia[4]. He buttoned his thin coat against the chilling wind.

In a cigar store he saw a well-dressed man lighting a cigar at a swinging light. His silk umbrella he had set by the door on entering. Soapy stepped inside, secured the umbrella and sauntered off with it slowly. The man at the cigar light followed hastily.

"My umbrella," he said, sternly.

"Oh, is it?" sneered Soapy, adding insult to petit larceny. "Well, why don't you call a policeman? I took it. Your umbrella! Why don't you call a cop? There stands one on the corner."

The umbrella owner slowed his steps. Soapy did likewise, with a feeling that luck would again run against him. The policeman looked at the two curiously.

"Of course," said the umbrella man—"that is—well, you know how these mistakes occur—I—if it's your umbrella I hope you'll excuse me—I picked it up this morning in a restaurant—If you recognize it as yours, why—I hope you'll—"

"Of course it's mine," said Soapy, viciously.

The ex-umbrella man retreated. The policeman hurried to assist a tall blonde in an opera cloak across the street in front of a street car that was approaching two blocks away.

Soapy walked eastward through a street damaged by improvements. He hurled the umbrella wrathfully into an excavation. He muttered against the men who wear helmets and carry clubs. Because he wanted to fall into their clutches, they seemed to regard him as a king who could do no wrong.

At length Soapy reached one of the avenues to the east where the glitter and turmoil were but faint. He set his face

[4] Arcadia: any region of simple peace and quiet.

down this toward Madison Square, for the homing instinct survives even when the home is a park bench.

But on an unusually quiet corner Soapy came to a standstill. Here was an old church, quaint and rambling and gabled. Through one violet-stained window a soft light glowed, where, no doubt, the organist loitered over the keys, making sure of his mastery of the coming Sabbath anthem. For there drifted out to Soapy's ears sweet music that caught and held him transfixed against the iron fence.

The moon was above, bright and serene; vehicles and pedestrians were few; sparrows twitted sleepily in the eaves—for a little while the scene might have been a country churchyard. And the anthem that the organist played cemented Soapy to the iron fence, for he had known it well in the days when his life contained such things as mothers and roses and ambitions and friends and immaculate thoughts and collars.

7

The conjunction of Soapy's receptive state of mind and the influences about the old church caused a sudden and wonderful change in his soul. He viewed with swift horror the pit into which he had tumbled, the degraded days, unworthy desires, dead hopes, wrecked faculties, and base motives that made up his life.

And also in a moment his heart responded thrillingly to this novel mood. An instantaneous and strong impulse moved him to battle with his desperate fate. He would pull himself out of the mire; he would make a man of himself again; he would conquer the evil that had taken possession of him. There was time; he was comparatively young yet: he would resurrect his old eager ambitions and pursue them without faltering. Those solemn but sweet organ notes had set up a revolution in him. Tomorrow he would go into the roaring downtown district and find work. A fur importer had once offered him a place as driver. He would find him tomorrow and ask for the position. He would be somebody in the world. He would—

Soapy felt a hand laid on his arm. He looked quickly around into the broad face of a policeman.

"What are you doin' here?" asked the officer.

"Nothing," said Soapy.

"Then come along," said the policeman.

"Three months on the Island," said the Magistrate in the Police Court the next morning.

The Skylight Room

Who ever heard of a star called Billy Jackson? That was the one Miss Leeson could see from her dark little room. Until one night—

First Mrs. Parker would show you the double parlors. You would not dare to interrupt her description of their advantages and of the merits of the gentleman who had occupied them for eight years. Then you would manage to stammer forth the confession that you were neither a doctor nor a dentist. Mrs. Parker's manner of receiving the admission was such that you could never afterward entertain the same feeling toward your parents, who had neglected to train you up in one of the professions that fitted Mrs. Parker's parlors.

Next you ascended one flight of stairs and looked at the second-floor-back at $8. Convinced by her second-floor manner that it was worth the $12 that Mr. Toosenberry always paid for it until he left to take charge of his brother's orange grove in Florida near Palm Beach, where Mrs. McIntyre always spent the winters that had the double front room with private bath, you managed to babble that you wanted something still cheaper.

If you survived Mrs. Parker's scorn, you were taken to look at Mr. Skidder's large hall room on the third floor. Mr. Skidder's room was not vacant. He wrote plays and smoked cigarettes in it all day long. But every room-hunter was made to visit his room to admire the lambrequins[1]. After each

---

[1] Lambrequins: draperies usually used on mantels.

visit, Mr. Skidder, from the fright caused by possible eviction, would pay something on his rent.

Then—oh, then—if you still stood on one foot, with your hot hand clutching the three moist dollars in your pocket, and hoarsely proclaimed your hideous poverty, nevermore would Mrs. Parker be cicerone[2] of yours. She would honk loudly the word "Clara," she would show you her back, and march downstairs. Then Clara, the maid, would escort you up the carpeted ladder that served for the fourth flight and show you the Skylight Room. It occupied 7 x 8 feet of floor space in the middle of the hall. On each side of it was a dark lumber closet or storeroom.

In it was an iron cot, a washstand, and a chair. A shelf was the dresser. Its four bare walls seemed to close in upon you like the sides of a coffin. Your hand crept to your throat, you gasped, you looked up as from a well—and breathed once more. Through the glass of the little skylight you saw a square of blue infinity.

"Two dollars, suh," Clara would say in her half-contemptuous tones.

One day Miss Leeson came hunting for a room. She carried a typewriter made to be lugged around by a much larger lady. She was a very little girl, with eyes and hair that had kept on growing after she had stopped and that always looked as if they were saying: "Goodness me! Why didn't you keep up with us?"

Mrs. Parker showed her the double parlors. "In this closet," she said, "one could keep a skeleton or anaesthetic or coal—"

"But I am neither a doctor nor a dentist," said Miss Leeson, with a shiver.

Mrs. Parker gave her the pitying, sneering, icy stare that she kept for those who failed to qualify as doctors or dentists, and led the way to the second-floor-back.

[2] Cicerone: an Italian guide.

"Eight dollars?" said Miss Leeson. "Dear me! I'm not Hetty[3] if I do look green. I'm just a poor little working girl. Show me something higher and lower."

Mr. Skidder jumped and strewed the floor with cigarette stubs at the rap on his door.

"Excuse me, Mr. Skidder," said Mrs. Parker, with her demon's smile at his pale looks. "I didn't know you were in. I asked the lady to have a look at your lambrequins."

"They're too lovely for anything," said Miss Leeson, smiling in exactly the way the angels do.

[3] Hetty: Hetty Green, an American millionairess, who lived from 1835 to 1916.

After they had gone Mr. Skidder got very busy erasing the tall, black-haired heroine from his latest (unproduced) play and inserted a small, roguish one with heavy, bright hair, and vivacious features.

"Anna Held[4] will jump at it," said Mr. Skidder to himself, putting his feet up against the lambrequins and disappearing in a cloud of smoke like an aerial cuttlefish.

Presently the call of "Clara!" sounded to the world the state of Miss Leeson's purse. A goblin seized her, mounted a stairway, thrust her into a vault with a glimmer of light in its top and muttered the menacing words "Two dollars!"

"I'll take it!" sighed Miss Leeson, sinking down upon the squeaky iron bed.

Every day Miss Leeson went out to work. At night she brought home papers with handwriting on them and made copies with her typewriter. Sometimes she had no work at night, and then she would sit on the steps of the high stoop with the other roomers. Miss Leeson was not intended for a skylight room when the plans were drawn for her creation. She was gay hearted and full of tender fancies. Once she let Mr. Skidder read to her three acts of his great (unpublished) comedy, "It's No Kid! or The Heir of the Subway."

There was rejoicing among the gentlemen roomers whenever Miss Leeson had time to sit on the steps for an hour or two. But Miss Longnecker, the tall blonde who taught in a public school and said, "Well, really!" to everything you said, sat on the top step and sniffed. And Miss Dorn, who shot at the moving ducks at Coney every Sunday and worked in a department store, sat on the bottom step and sniffed. Miss Leeson sat on the middle step and the men would quickly group around her.

Especially Mr. Skidder, who had cast her in his mind for the star part in a private, romantic (unspoken) drama in real life. And especially Mr. Hoover, who was forty-five, fat, flush, and foolish. And especially very young Mr. Evans,

[4] Anna Held: an actress famous in O. Henry's time.

who set up a hollow cough to induce her to ask him to leave off cigarettes. The men voted her "the funniest and jolliest ever," but the sniffs on the top step and the lower step were unforgiving.

. . . .

I pray you let the drama halt while Chorus stalks to the footlights and drops an epicedian[5] tear upon the fatness of Mr. Hoover. Tune the pipes to the tragedy of tallow, the bane of bulk, the calamity of corpulence. Tried out, Falstaff[6] might have rendered more romance to the ton than would have Romeo's[7] rickety ribs to the ounce. A lover may sigh, but he must not puff. To the train of Momus[8] are the fat men remanded. In vain beats faithfullest heart above a 52-inch belt. Away, Hoover! Hoover, forty-five, flush and foolish, might carry off Helen[9] herself; Hoover, forty-five, flush, foolish, and fat is meat for perdition. There was never a chance for you, Hoover.

As Mrs. Parker's roomers sat thus one summer's evening, Miss Leeson looked up into the firmament and cried with her little gay laugh:

"Why, there's Billy Jackson! I can see him from down here, too."

All looked up—some at the windows of skyscrapers, some casting about for an airship, Jackson-guided.

"It's that star," explained Miss Leeson, pointing with a tiny finger. "Not the big one that twinkles—the steady blue one near it. I can see it every night through my skylight. I named it Billy Jackson."

"Well, really!" said Miss Longnecker. "I didn't know you were an astronomer, Miss Leeson."

"Oh, yes," said the small star gazer, "I know as much as

[5] Epicedian: pertaining to a funeral ode or dirge.

[6] Falstaff: a fat, jolly character in three of Shakespeare's plays.

[7] Romeo: the hero of Shakespeare's play, *Romeo and Juliet*.

[8] Momus: the Greek god of mockery and fault-finding.

[9] Helen: a beautiful Grecian woman who was the indirect cause of the Trojan War.

any of them about the style of sleeves they're going to wear next fall in Mars."

"Well, really!" said Miss Longnecker. "The star you refer to is Gamma, of the constellation Cassiopeia. It is nearly of the second magnitude, and its meridian passage is—"

"Oh," said the very young Mr. Evans, "I think Billy Jackson is a much better name for it."

"Same here," said Mr. Hoover, loudly breathing defiance to Miss Longnecker. "I think Miss Leeson has just as much right to name stars as any of those astrologers had."

"Well, really!" said Miss Longnecker.

"I wonder whether it's a shooting star," remarked Miss Dorn. "I hit nine ducks and a rabbit out of ten in the gallery at Coney Sunday."

"He doesn't show up very well from down here," said Miss Leeson. "You ought to see him from my room. You know you can see stars even in the daytime from the bottom of a well. At night my room is like the shaft of a coal mine, and it makes Billy Jackson look like the big diamond pin that Night fastens her kimono with."

There came a time after that when Miss Leeson brought no papers home to copy. And when she went out in the morning instead of working she went from office to office and let her heart melt away in the drip of cold refusals transmitted through insolent office boys. This went on.

There came an evening when she wearily climbed Mrs. Parker's stoop at the hour when she always returned from her dinner at the restaurant. But she had had no dinner.

As she stepped into the hall Mr. Hoover met her and seized his chance. He asked her to marry him, and his fatness hovered above her like an avalanche. She dodged, and caught the balustrade. He tried for her hand, and she raised it and smote him weakly in the face. Step by step she went up, dragging herself by the railing. She passed Mr. Skidder's door as he was red-inking a stage direction for Myrtle Delorme (Miss Leeson) in his (unaccepted) comedy, to "dance across stage from L to the side of the Count." Up the carpeted ladder she crawled at last and opened the door of the skylight room.

She was too weak to light the lamp or to undress. She fell upon the iron cot, her fragile body scarcely hollowing the worn springs. And in that Erebus[10] of a room she slowly raised her heavy eyelids, and smiled.

For Billy Jackson was shining down on her, calm and bright and constant through the skylight. There was no world about her. She was sunk in a pit of blackness, with but that small square of pallid light framing the star that she had so playfully and oh, so ineffectually, named. Miss Longnecker must be right: it was Gamma, of the constellation Cassiopeia, and not Billy Jackson. And yet she could not let it be Gamma.

As she lay on her back, she tried twice to raise her arm. The third time she got two thin fingers to her lips and blew a kiss out of the black pit to Billy Jackson. Her arm fell back limply.

"Good-by, Billy," she murmured, faintly. "You're millions of miles away and you won't even twinkle once. But you kept where I could see you most of the time up there when there wasn't anything else but darkness to look at, didn't you? . . . Millions of miles. . . . Good-by, Billy Jackson."

Clara, the maid, found the door locked at 10 the next day, and they forced it open. Vinegar, and the slapping of wrists and burnt feathers proving of no avail, some one ran to phone for an ambulance.

In due time it backed up to the door with much gong-clanging, and the capable young medico, in his white linen coat, ready, active, confident, with his smooth face half smiling, half grim, danced up the steps.

"Ambulance call to 49," he said, briefly. "What's the trouble?"

[10] Erebus: among the ancient Greeks and Romans a dark place between heaven and hell.

"Oh, yes, doctor," sniffed Mrs. Parker, as though her trouble that there should be trouble in the house was the greater. "I can't think what can be the matter with her. Nothing we could do would bring her to. It's a young woman, Miss Elsie—yes, a Miss Elsie Leeson. Never before in my house—"

"What room?" cried the doctor in a terrible voice, to which Mrs. Parker was a stranger.

"The skylight room. It—"

Evidently the ambulance doctor was familiar with the location of skylight rooms. He was gone up the stairs four at a time. Mrs. Parker followed slowly, as her dignity demanded.

On the first landing she met him coming back bearing the astronomer in his arms. He stopped and let loose his tongue, not loudly. Gradually Mrs. Parker crumpled as a stiff garment that slips down from a nail. Ever afterwards there remained crumples in her mind and body. Sometimes her curious roomers would ask her what the doctor said to her.

"Let that be," she would answer. "If I can get forgiveness for having heard it I will be satisified."

The ambulance physician strode with his burden through the pack of hounds that follow the curiosity chase, and even they fell back along the sidewalk abashed, for his face was that of one who bears his own dead.

They noticed that he did not lay down upon the bed prepared for it in the ambulance the form that he carried, and all that he said was: "Drive like the devil, Wilson," to the driver.

That is all. Is it a story? In the next morning's paper I saw a little news item, and the last sentence of it may help you (as it helped me) to weld the incidents together.

It recounted the reception in Bellevue Hospital of a young woman who had been removed from No. 49 East—Street, suffering from starvation. It concluded with these words:

"Dr. William Jackson, the ambulance physician who attended the case, says the patient will recover."

Mammon[1] and the Archer

Maybe you've been in lots of traffic jams. Have you ever seen one put to such good use?

Old Anthony Rockwall, retired manufacturer and proprietor of Rockwall's Eureka Soap, looked out the library window of his Fifth Avenue mansion and grinned. His neighbor to the right—the aristocratic clubman, G. Van Schuylight Suffolk-Jones—came out to his waiting motor-car, wrinkling a contumelious[2] nostril as usual, at the Italian renaissance sculpture of the soap palace's front elevation.

"Stuck-up old statuette of nothing doing!" commented the ex-Soap King. "The Eden Musée[3] will get that old frozen Nesselrode[4] yet if he don't watch out. I'll have this house painted red, white, and blue next summer and see if that'll make his Dutch nose turn up any higher."

And then Anthony Rockwall, who never cared for bells, went to the door of his library and shouted "Mike!" in the same voice that had once chipped off pieces of the sod on the Kansas prairies.

"Tell my son," said Anthony to the answering servant, "to come in here before he leaves the house."

When young Rockwall entered the library the old man laid aside his newspaper, looked at him with a kindly grimness on his big, smooth, ruddy face, rumpled his mop of white hair

[1] Mammon: the ancient Syrian god of wealth.
[2] Contumelious: scornful.
[3] Eden Musée: a private museum in New York noted in the early 1900s for its wax figures of famous people.
[4] Nesselrode: a frozen pudding.

with one hand and rattled the keys in his pocket with the other.

"Richard," said Anthony Rockwall, "what do you pay for the soap that you use?"

Richard, only six months home from college, was startled a little. He had not yet taken the measure of this sire of his, who was as full of unexpectedness as a girl at her first party.

"Six dollars a dozen, I think, Dad."

"And your clothes?"

"I suppose about sixty dollars, as a rule."

"You're a gentleman," said Anthony, decidedly. "I've heard of these young bloods spending $24 a dozen for soap, and going over the hundred mark for clothes. You've got as much money to waste as any of 'em, and yet you stick to what's decent and moderate. Now I use the old Eureka—not only for sentiment, but it's the purest soap made. Whenever you pay more than 10 cents a cake for soap you buy bad perfumes and labels. But 50 cents is doing very well for a young man in your generation, position, and condition. As I said, you're a gentleman. They say it takes three generations to make one. They're off. Money'll do it as slick as soap grease. It's made you one. By hokey! it's almost made one of me. I'm nearly as impolite and disagreeable and ill-mannered as these two old gents on each side of me that can't sleep of nights because I bought in between 'em."

"There are some things that money can't accomplish," remarked young Rockwall, rather gloomily.

"Now, don't say that," said old Anthony, shocked. "I bet my money on money every time. I've been through the encyclopedia down to Y looking for something you can't buy with it; and I expect to have to take up the appendix next week. I'm for money against the field. Tell me something money won't buy."

"For one thing," answered Richard, rankling a little, "it won't buy one into the exclusive circles of society."

"Oho! won't it?" thundered the champion of the root of evil. "You tell me where your exclusive circles would be if the first Astor hadn't had money to pay for his steerage passage over?"

Richard sighed.

"And that's what I was coming to," said the old man, less boisterously. "That's why I asked you to come in. There's something going wrong with you, boy. I've been noticing it for two weeks. Out with it. I guess I could lay my hands on eleven millions within twenty-four hours, besides the real estate. If it's your liver, there's the *Rambler* down in the bay, coaled, and ready to steam down to the Bahamas in two days."

"Not a bad guess, Dad; you haven't missed it far."

"Ah," said Anthony, keenly; "what's her name?"

Richard began to walk up and down the library floor. There was enough comradeship and sympathy in this crude old father of his to draw his confidence.

"Why don't you ask her?" demanded old Anthony. "She'll jump at you. You've got the money and the looks, and you're a decent boy. Your hands are clean. You've got no Eureka soap on 'em. You've been to college, but she'll overlook that."

"I haven't had a chance," said Richard.

"Make one," said Anthony. "Take her for a walk in the park, or a ride, or walk home with her from church. Chance! Pshaw!"

"You don't know the social mill, Dad. She's part of the stream that turns it. Every hour and minute of her time is arranged for days in advance. I must have that girl, Dad, or this town is a blackjack swamp forevermore. And I can't write it—I can't do that."

"Tut!" said the old man. "Do you mean to tell me that with all the money I've got you can't get an hour or two of a girl's time for yourself?"

"I've put it off too late. She's going to sail for Europe at noon day after tomorrow for a two years' stay. I'm to see her alone tomorrow evening for a few minutes. She's at Larchmont now at her aunt's. I can't go there. But I'm allowed to meet her with a cab at the Grand Central Station tomorrow evening at the 8:30 train. We drive down Broadway to Wallack's at a gallop, where her mother and a box party will be waiting for us in the lobby. Do you think she would listen to a declaration from me during that six or eight minutes under those circumstances? No. And what chance would I have in the theater or afterward? None. No, Dad, this is one tangle that your money can't unravel. We can't buy one minute of time with cash; if we could, rich people would live longer. There's no hope of getting a talk with Miss Lantry before she sails."

"All right, Richard, my boy," said old Anthony, cheerfully. "You may run along down to your club now. I'm glad it ain't your liver. But don't forget to burn a few punk sticks in the joss house to the great god Mazuma from time to time. You say money won't buy time? Well, of course, you can't order eternity wrapped up and delivered at your residence for a price, but I've seen Father Time get pretty bad stone bruises on his heels when he walked through the gold diggings."

That night came Aunt Ellen, gentle, sentimental, wrinkled, sighing, oppressed by wealth, in to Brother Anthony at his evening paper, and began to talk on the subject of lovers' woes.

"He told me all about it," said Brother Anthony, yawning. "I told him my bank account was at his service. And then he began to knock money. Said money couldn't help. Said the rules of society couldn't be bucked for a yard by a team of ten millionaires."

"Oh, Anthony," sighed Aunt Ellen, "I wish you would not think so much of money. Wealth is nothing where a true affection is concerned. Love is all-powerful. If he only had spoken earlier! She could not have refused our Richard. But now I fear it is too late. He will have no opportunity to address her. All your gold cannot bring happiness to your son."

At eight o'clock the next evening Aunt Ellen took a quaint old gold ring from a moth-eaten case and gave it to Richard.

"Wear it tonight, nephew," she begged. "Your mother gave it to me. Good Luck in love she said it brought. She asked me to give it to you when you find the one you loved."

Young Rockwall took the ring reverently and tried it on his smallest finger. It slipped as far as the second joint and stopped. He took it off and stuffed it into his vest pocket, after the manner of man. And then he phoned for his cab.

At the station he captured Miss Lantry out of the gabbing mob at eight thirty-two.

"We mustn't keep mamma and the others waiting," said she.

"To Wallack's Theater as fast as you can drive!" said Richard, loyally.

They whirled up Forty-second to Broadway, and then down the white-starred lane that leads from the soft meadows of sunset to the rocky hills of morning.

At Thirty-fourth Street young Richard quickly thrust up the trap and ordered the cabman to stop.

"I've dropped a ring," he apologized, as he climbed out. "It was my mother's, and I'd hate to lose it. I won't detain you a minute—I saw where it fell."

In less than a minute he was back in the cab with the ring.

But within that minute a crosstown car had stopped directly in front of the cab. The cabman tried to pass to the left, but a heavy express wagon cut him off. He tried the right and had to back away from a furniture van that had no business to be there. He tried to back out, but dropped his reins and swore dutifully. He was blockaded in a tangled mess of vehicles and horses.

One of those street blockades had occurred that sometimes

tie up commerce and movement quite suddenly in the big city.

"Why don't you drive on?" said Miss Lantry impatiently. "We'll be late."

Richard stood up in the cab and looked around. He saw a congested flood of wagons, trucks, cabs, vans, and street cars filling the vast space where Broadway, Sixth Avenue, and Thirty-fourth Street cross one another as a twenty-six inch maiden fills her twenty-two inch girdle. And still from all the cross streets they were hurrying and rattling toward the converging point at full speed, and hurling themselves into the straggling mass, locking wheels and adding their cries and curses to the clamor. The entire traffic of Manhattan seemed to have jammed itself around them. The oldest New Yorker among the thousands of spectators that lined the sidewalks had not witnessed a street blockade of the proportions of this one.

"I'm very sorry," said Richard, as he resumed his seat, "but it looks as if we are stuck. They won't get this jumble loosened up in an hour. It was my fault. If I hadn't dropped the ring we—"

"Let me see the ring," said Miss Lantry. "Now that it can't be helped, I don't care. I think theaters are stupid, anyway."

At 11 o'clock that night somebody tapped lightly on Anthony Rockwall's door.

"Come in," shouted Anthony, who was in a red dressing-gown, reading a book of piratical adventures.

Somebody was Aunt Ellen, looking like a gray-haired angel that had been left on earth by mistake.

"They're engaged, Anthony," she said, softly. "She has promised to marry our Richard. On their way to the theater there was a street blockade, and it was two hours before their cab could get out of it.

"And oh, Brother Anthony, don't ever boast of the power of money again. A little emblem of true love—a little ring that symbolized unending and unmercenary affection—was the cause of our Richard finding his happiness. He dropped it in the street, and got out to recover it. And before they could continue the blockade occurred. He spoke to his love and won her there while the cab was hemmed in. Money is nothing compared with true love, Anthony."

"All right," said old Anthony. "I'm glad the boy has got what he wanted. I told him I wouldn't spare any expense in the matter if—"

"But Brother Anthony, what good could your money have done?"

"Sister," said Anthony Rockwall, "I've got my pirate in a devil of a scrape. His ship has just been scuttled, and he's too good a judge of the value of money to let drown. I wish you would let me go on with this chapter."

The story should end here. I wish it would as heartily as you who read it wish it did. But we must go to the bottom of the well for truth.

The next day a person with red hands and a blue polka-dot necktie, who called himself Kelly, called at Anthony Rockwall's house, and was at once received in the library.

"Well," said Anthony, reaching for his check-book, "it was a good bilin' of soap. Let's see—you had $5,000 in cash."

"I paid out $300 more of my own," said Kelly. "I had to go a little above the estimate. I got the express wagons and cabs mostly for $5; but the trucks and two-horse teams mostly raised me to $10. The motormen wanted $10, and some of the loaded teams $20. The cops struck me hardest—$50 I paid two and the rest $20 and $25. But didn't it work beautiful, Mr. Rockwall? I'm glad William A. Brady[5] wasn't onto that little outdoor vehicle mob scene, I wouldn't want William to break his heart with jealousy. And never a rehearsal, either! The boys was on time to the fraction of a second. It was two hours before a snake could get below Greeley's statue."

"Thirteen hundred—there you are, Kelly," said Anthony, tearing off a check. "Your thousand, and the $300 you were out. You don't despise money, do you, Kelly?"

"Me?" said Kelly. "I can lick the man that invented poverty."

Anthony called Kelly when he was at the door.

"You didn't notice," said he, "anywhere in the tieup, a kind of a fat boy without any clothes on shooting arrows around with a bow, did you?"

"Why, no," said Kelly, mystified. "I didn't. If he was like you say, maybe the cops pinched him before I got there."

"I thought the little rascal wouldn't be on hand," chuckled Anthony. "Good-by, Kelly."

---

[5] William A. Brady: an American theater manager.

The Gift of the Magi[1]

The Three Wise Men brought valuable gifts to the Christ Child. Della and Jim had something much more precious to give each other.

One dollar and eighty-seven cents. That was all. And sixty cents of it was in pennies. Pennies saved one and two at a time by bulldozing the grocer and the vegetable man and the butcher until one's cheeks burned with shame. Three times Della counted it. One dollar and eighty-seven cents. And the next day would be Christmas.

There was clearly nothing to do but flop down on the shabby little couch and howl. So Della did it. This brings the moral reflection that life is made up of sobs, sniffles, and smiles, with sniffles predominating.

While the mistress of the home is gradually subsiding from the first stage to the second, take a look at the home. A furnished flat at $8 per week. It did not exactly beggar description, but it certainly looked poor.

In the vestibule below was a letter-box into which no letter would go, and an electric button from which no mortal finger could coax a ring. Also there was a card bearing the name "Mr. James Dillingham Young."

The "Dillingham" had been flung to the breeze during a former period of prosperity when its possessor was being paid $30 per week. Now, when the income was shrunk to $20, the letters of "Dillingham" looked blurred, as though they

---

[1] The Magi: The Three Wise Men who, according to the Bible, brought gifts to the Christ Child.

were thinking seriously of contracting to a modest and un-assuming D. But whenever Mr. James Dillingham Young came home and reached his flat above he was called "Jim" and greatly hugged by Mrs. James Dillingham Young, already introduced to you as Della. Which is all very good.

Della finished her cry and attended to her cheeks with the powder rag. She stood by the window and looked out dully at a gray cat walking a gray fence in a gray backyard. Tomorrow would be Christmas Day, and she had only $1.87 with which to buy Jim a present. She had been saving every penny she could for months, with this result. Twenty dollars a week doesn't go far. Expenses had been greater than she had calculated. They always are. Only $1.87 to buy a present for Jim. Her Jim. Many a happy hour she spent planning for something nice for him. Something fine and rare and sterling—something just a little bit near to being worthy of the honor of being owned by Jim.

There was a pier-glass between the windows of the room. Perhaps you have seen a pier-glass in an $8 flat. A very thin and very agile person may, by observing his reflection in a rapid sequence of strips, obtain a fairly accurate conception of his looks. Della, being slender, had mastered the art.

Suddenly she whirled from the window and stood before the glass. Her eyes were shining brilliantly, but her face had lost its color within twenty seconds. Rapidly she pulled down her hair and let it fall to its full length.

Now, there were two possessions of the James Dillingham Youngs in which they both took a mighty pride. One was Jim's gold watch that had been his father's and his grand-father's. The other was Della's hair. Had the Queen of Sheba lived in the flat across the airshaft, Della would have let her hair hang out the window some day to dry just to mock Her Majesty's jewels and gifts. Had King Solomon been the janitor, with all his treasures piled up in the basement, Jim would have pulled out his watch every time he passed, just to see him pluck at his beard from envy.

So now Della's beautiful hair fell about her rippling and

shining like a cascade of brown waters. It reached below her knee and made itself almost a garment for her. And then she did it up again nervously and quickly. Once she faltered for a minute and stood still while a tear or two splashed on the worn red carpet.

On went her old brown jacket; on went her old brown hat. With a whirl of skirts and with the brilliant sparkle still in her eyes, she fluttered out the door and down the stairs to the street.

Where she stopped the sign read: "Mme Sofronie. Hair Goods of All Kinds." One flight up Della ran, and collected herself, panting. Madame, large, too white, chilly, hardly looked the "Sofronie."

"Will you buy my hair?" asked Della.

"I buy hair," said Madame. "Take yer hat off and let's have a sight at the looks of it."

Down rippled the brown cascade.

"Twenty dollars," said Madame, lifting the mass with a practiced hand.

"Give it to me quick," said Della.

Oh, and the next two hours tripped by on rosy wings. She was ransacking the stores for Jim's present.

She found it at last. It surely had been made for Jim and no one else. There was no other like it in any of the stores, and she had turned all of them inside out. It was a platinum fob chain simple and chaste in design, properly proclaiming its value by substance alone and not by ornamentation—as all good things should do. It was even worthy of The Watch. As soon as she saw it she knew that it must be Jim's. It was like him. Quietness and value—the description applied to both. Twenty-one dollars they took from her for it, and she hurried home with the 87 cents. With that chain on his watch Jim might be properly anxious about the time in any company. Grand as the watch was, he sometimes looked at it on the sly on account of the old leather strap that he used in place of a chain.

When Della reached home her joy gave way a little to

prudence and reason. She got out her curling irons and lighted the gas and went to work.

Within forty minutes her head was covered with tiny, close-lying curls that made her look wonderfully like a truant schoolboy. She looked at her reflection in the mirror long, carefully, and critically.

"If Jim doesn't kill me," she said to herself, "before he takes a second look at me, he'll say I look like a Coney Island chorus girl. But what could I do—oh! what could I do with $1.87?"

At 7 o'clock the coffee was made and the frying pan was on the back of the stove hot and ready to cook the chops.

Jim was never late. Della doubled the fob chain in her hand and sat on the corner of the table near the door that he always entered. Then she heard his step on the stair away down on the first flight, and she turned white for just a moment. She had a habit of saying silent prayers about the simplest everyday things, and now she whispered: "Please God, make him think I am still pretty."

The door opened and Jim stepped in and closed it. He looked thin and very serious. Poor fellow, he was only twenty-two—and to be burdened with a family! He needed a new overcoat and he was without gloves.

Jim stopped inside the door, as immovable as a setter at the scent of quail. His eyes were fixed upon Della, and there was an expression in them that she could not read, and it terrified her. It was not anger, nor surprise, nor disapproval, nor horror, nor any of the sentiments that she had been prepared for. He simply stared at her fixedly with that peculiar expression on his face.

Della wiggled off the table and went for him.

"Jim, darling," she cried, "don't look at me that way. I had my hair cut off and sold it because I couldn't have lived through Christmas without giving you a present. It'll grow out again—you won't mind, will you? I just had to do it. My hair grows awfully fast. Say 'Merry Christmas!' Jim, and

let's be happy. You don't know what a nice—what a beautiful, nice gift I've got for you."

"You've cut off your hair?" asked Jim.

"Cut it off and sold it," said Della. "Don't you like me just as well, anyhow? I'm me without my hair, ain't I?"

Jim looked about the room curiously.

"You say your hair is gone?" he said, with an air almost of idiocy.

"You needn't look for it," said Della. "It's sold, I tell you—sold and gone, too. It's Christmas Eve, boy. Be good to me, for it went for you. Maybe the hairs of my head were numbered," she went on with a sudden serious sweetness, "but nobody could ever count my love for you. Shall I put the chops on, Jim?"

Out of his trance Jim seemed quickly to wake. He enfolded his Della. For ten seconds let us regard with discreet scrutiny some object in the other direction. Eight dollars a week or a million a year—what is the difference? A mathematician or a wit would give you the wrong answer. The magi brought valuable gifts, but that was not among them. This dark assertion will be illuminated later on.

Jim drew a package from his overcoat pocket and threw it upon the table.

"Don't make any mistake, Dell," he said, "about me. I don't think there's anything in the way of a haircut or a shave or a shampoo that could make me like my girl any less. But if you'll unwrap that package you may see why you had me going a while at first."

White and nimble fingers tore at the string and paper. And then an ecstatic scream of joy; and then, alas! a quick feminine change to hysterical tears and wails.

For there lay The Combs—the set of combs, side and back, that Della had worshipped for long in a Broadway window. Beautiful combs, pure tortoise shell, with jewelled rims—just the shade to wear in the beautiful vanished hair. They were expensive combs, she knew, and her heart had simply craved and yearned over them without the least hope of possession. And now, they were hers, but the tresses that should have adorned the coveted adornments were gone.

But she hugged them to her bosom, and at length she was able to look up with dim eyes and smile and say: "My hair grows so fast, Jim!"

And then Della leaped up like a little singed cat and cried, "Oh, oh!"

Jim had not yet seen his beautiful present. She held it out to him eagerly upon her open palm. The dull precious metal seemed to flash with a reflection of her bright and ardent spirit.

"Isn't it a dandy, Jim? I hunted all over town to find it. You'll have to look at the time a hundred times a day now. Give me your watch. I want to see how it looks on it."

Instead of obeying, Jim tumbled down on the couch and put his hands under the back of his head and smiled.

"Dell," said he, "let's put our Christmas presents away and keep 'em a while. They're too nice to use just at present. I sold the watch to get the money to buy your combs. And now suppose you put the chops on."

The Magi, as you know, were wise men—wonderfully wise men—who brought gifts to the Babe in the manger. They invented the art of giving Christmas presents. Being wise, their gifts were no doubt wise ones, possibly bearing the privilege of exchange in case of duplication. And here I have lamely related to you the uneventful story of two foolish children in a flat who most unwisely sacrificed for each other the greatest treasures of their house. But in a last word to the wise of these days let it be said that of all who give and receive gifts, such as they are wisest. Everywhere they are wisest. They are the Magi.

Springtime à La Carte

New York is a big city; but with the help of dandelions and a typewriter the farmer found his way around in it.

It was a day in March.

Never, never begin a story this way when you write one. No opening could possibly be worse. It is unimaginative, flat, dry, and likely to consist of mere wind. But in this instance it is allowable. For the following paragraph, which should have started the narrative, is too wild to be flaunted in the face of the reader without preparation.

Sarah was crying over her bill of fare.

Think of a New York girl shedding tears on the menu card!

To account for this you will be allowed to guess that the lobsters were all out, or that she had sworn off ice-cream during Lent, or that she had ordered onions, or that she had just come from a matinée. And then, all these theories being wrong, you will please let the story proceed.

The gentleman who announced that the world was an oyster which he with his sword would open made a larger hit than he deserved. It is not difficult to open an oyster with a sword. But did you ever notice anyone try to open the worldly oyster with a typewriter? Like to wait for a dozen raw opened that way?

Sarah had managed to pry apart the shells with her unhandy weapon far enough to nibble a wee bit at the cold and clammy world within. She knew no more shorthand than if she had been a graduate in stenography just let slip upon the world by a business college. So, not being able to stenog, she could not enter that bright world of office talent. She was a freelance typist and canvassed for odd jobs of copying.

The most brilliant and crowning feat of Sarah's battle with the world was the deal she made with Schulenberg's Home Restaurant. The restaurant was next door to the old red brick in which she roomed. One evening after dining at Schulenberg's 40-cent, five-course *table d'hote* (served as fast as you throw five baseballs) Sarah took away with her the bill of fare. It was written in an almost unreadable script neither English nor German, and so arranged that if you were not careful you began with a toothpick and rice pudding and ended with soup and the day of the week.

The next day Sarah showed Schulenberg a neat card on which the menu was beautifully typewritten with the food temptingly marshalled under their right and proper heads from "hors d'oeuvre" to "not responsible for overcoats and umbrellas."

Schulenberg became a naturalized citizen on the spot. Before Sarah left him she had him willingly committed to an agreement. She was to furnish typewritten bills of fare for the twenty-one tables in the restaurant—a new bill for each day's dinner, and new ones for breakfast and lunch as often as changes occurred in the food or as neatness required.

In return for this Schulenberg was to send three meals per diem to Sarah's hall room—and furnish her each afternoon with a pencil draft of what Fate had in store for Schulenberg's customers on the morrow.

Mutual satisfaction resulted from the agreement. Schulenberg's patrons now knew what the food they ate was called even if its nature sometimes puzzled them. And Sarah had food during a cold, dull winter, which was the main thing with her.

And then the almanac lied, and said that spring had come. Spring comes when it comes. The frozen snows of January still lay in the cross-town streets. The hand organs still played "In the Good Old Summertime," with their December vivacity and expression. Men began to make thirty-day notes to buy Easter dresses. Janitors shut off steam. And when these things happen one may know that the city is still in the clutches of winter.

One afternoon Sarah shivered in her elegant hall bedroom. She had no work to do except Schulenberg's menu cards. Sarah sat in her squeaky willow rocker, and looked out the window. The calendar on the wall kept crying to her: "Springtime is here, Sarah—springtime is here, I tell you. Look at me, Sarah, my figures show it. You've got a neat figure yourself, Sarah—a—nice springtime figure—why do you look out the window so sadly?"

Sarah's room was at the back of the house. Looking out the window she could see the windowless rear brick wall of the box factory on the next street. But the wall was clearest crystal; and Sarah was looking down a grassy lane shaded with cherry trees and elms and bordered with raspberry bushes and Cherokee roses.

Spring's real signs are too subtle for the eye and ear. Some must have the flowering crocus, the wood-starring dogwood, the voice of bluebird—even so gross a reminder as the farewell handshake of the retiring buckwheat and oyster before they can welcome the Lady in Green to their dull bosoms.

On the previous summer Sarah had gone into the country and loved a farmer.

Sarah stayed two weeks at Sunnybrook Farm. There she learned to love old Farmer Franklin's son Walter. Farmers have been loved and wedded and turned out to grass in less time. But young Walter Franklin was a modern farmer. He had a telephone in his cow house, and he could figure up exactly what effect next year's Canada wheat crop would have on potatoes planted in the dark of the moon.

It was in this shaded and raspberried lane that Walter

had wooed and won her. And together they had sat and
woven a crown of dandelions for her hair. He had immoder-
ately praised the effect of the yellow blossoms against her
brown tresses; and she had left the chaplet there, and walked
back to the house swinging her straw hat in her hands.

They were to marry in the spring—at the very first signs
of spring, Walter said. And Sarah came back to the city to
pound her typewriter.

A knock at the door dispelled Sarah's visions of that happy
day. A waiter had brought the rough pencil draft of the
Home Restaurant's next day fare in old Schulenberg's angular
hand.

Sarah sat down to her typewriter and slipped a card between the rollers. She was a nimble worker. Generally in an
hour and a half the twenty-one menu cards were written
and ready.

Today there were more changes on the bill of fare than
usual. The soups were lighter; pork was eliminated from the
entrées, figuring only with Russian turnips among the roasts.
The gracious spirit of spring could be seen in the entire
menu. Lamb, that lately capered on the greening hillsides,
was becoming exploited with the sauce that commemorated
its gambols. The song of the oyster, though not silenced, was
diminuendo con amore.[1] The frying pan seemed to be held,
inactive, behind the bars of the broiler. The pie list swelled;
the richer puddings had vanished; the sausage, with his
drapery wrapped about him, barely lingered in a pleasant
thanatopsis[2] with the buck wheats and the sweet but doomed
maple.

Sarah's fingers danced like midgets above a summer
stream. Down through the courses she worked, giving each
item its position according to its length with an accurate
eye.

[1] Diminuendo con amore: a musical term which is best translated
here as growing weaker though still a song to be loved.
[2] Thanatopsis: a song of death.

Just above the desserts came the list of vegetables. Carrots and peas, asparagus on toast, the usual tomatoes and corn, and succotash, lima beans, cabbage—and then—

Sarah was crying over her bill of fare. Tears from the depths of some divine despair rose in her heart and gathered to her eyes. Down went her head on the little typewriter stand; and the keyboard rattled a dry accompaniment to her moist sobs.

For she had received no letter from Walter in two weeks, and the next item on the bill of fare was—dandelions with some kind of egg—but bother the egg!—dandelions, with whose golden blooms Walter had crowned her his queen of love and future bride—dandelions, reminder of her happiest days.

Madam, I dare you to smile until you suffer this test: Let the roses that Percy brought you on the night you gave him your heart be served as a salad with French dressing before your eyes at a Schulenberg *table d'hôte.* Had Juliet[3] so seen her love tokens dishonored the sooner would she have sought the lethean herbs of the good apothecary.[4]

But what witch is Spring! Into the great cold city of stone and iron a message had to be sent. There was none to convey it but the little hardy courier of the fields with his rough green coat and modest air. He is a true soldier of fortune, this *dente-de-lion*—this lion's tooth, as the French chefs call him. Flowered, he will assist at love-making, wreathed in my lady's nut-brown hair; young and callow and unblossomed, he goes into the boiling pot and delivers the word of his sovereign mistress.

By and by Sarah forced back her tears. The cards must be written. But, still in a faint, golden glow from her dandelion dream, she fingered the typewriter keys absently for a little while, with her mind and heart in the meadow lane

[3] Juliet: the heroine of Shakespeare's play, *Romeo and Juliet.*

[4] Lethean herbs of the good apothecary: herbs given to Juliet to make her lose consciousness.

with her young farmer. But soon she came swiftly back to the rock-bound lanes of Manhattan, and the typewriter began to rattle and jump like a strike-breaker's motor car.

At 6 o'clock the waiter brought her dinner and carried away the typewritten bill of fare. When Sarah ate she set aside, with a sigh, the dish of dandelions. As this dark mass had been transformed from a bright and love-endorsed flower to be a common vegetable, so had her summer hopes wilted and perished. Love may, as Shakespeare said, feed on itself: but Sarah could not bring herself to eat the dandelions that had graced, as ornaments, the first spiritual banquet of her heart's true affection.

At 7:30 the couple in the next room began to quarrel: the man in the room above sought for A on his flute; the gas went a little lower; three coal wagons started to unload—the only sound of which the phonograph is jealous; cats on the back fences slowly retreated toward Mukden. By these signs Sarah knew that it was time for her to read. She got out *The Cloister and the Hearth,* the best non-selling book of the month, settled her feet on her trunk, and began to wander with Gerard.

The front door bell rang. The landlady answered it. Sarah left Gerard and Denys[5] treed by a bear and listened. Oh, yes; you would just as she did!

And then a strong voice was heard in the hall below, and Sarah jumped for her door.

You have guessed it. She reached the top of the stairs just as her farmer came up, three at a jump, and reaped and garnered her, with nothing left for the gleaners.

"Why haven't you written—oh, why?" cried Sarah.

"New York is a pretty large town," said Walter Franklin. "I came in a week ago to your old address. I found that you went away on a Thursday. That consoled some; it eliminated the possible Friday bad luck. But it didn't prevent my

[5] Gerard and Denys: characters in *The Cloister and the Hearth.*

hunting for you with police and otherwise ever since!"

"I wrote!" said Sarah, vehemently.

"Never got it!"

"Then how did you find me?"

The young farmer smiled a springtime smile.

"I dropped into that Home Restaurant next door this evening," said he. "I don't care who knows it. I like a dish of some kind of greens at this time of the year. I ran my eye down that nice typewritten bill of fare looking for something in that line. When I got below cabbage I turned my chair over and hollered for the proprietor. He told me where you lived."

"I remember," sighed Sarah, happily. "That was dandelions below cabbage."

"I'd know that cranky capital W 'way above the line that your typewriter makes anywhere in the world," said Franklin.

"Why, there's no W in dandelions," said Sarah in surprise.

The young man drew the bill of fare from his pocket and pointed to a line.

Sarah recognized the first card she had typewritten that afternoon. There was still the rayed splotch in the upper right-hand corner where a tear had fallen. But over the spot where one should have read the name of the meadow plant, the clinging memory of their golden blossoms had allowed her fingers to strike strange keys.

Between the red cabbage and the stuffed green peppers was the item:

"DEAREST WALTER, WITH HARD-BOILED EGG."

The Romance
of a
Busy Broker

Just how busy can you get? You've probably never heard of anyone so absent-minded as this business man.

Pitcher, confidential clerk in the office of Harvey Maxwell, broker, allowed a look of mild interest and surprise to visit his usually expressionless countenance when his employer briskly entered at half-past nine in company with his young lady stenographer. With a snappy "Good-morning, Pitcher," Maxwell dashed at his desk as though he were intending to leap over it, and then plunged into the great heap of letters and telegrams waiting there for him.

The young lady had been Maxwell's stenographer for a year. She was beautiful in a way that was decidedly unstenographic. She wore no chains, bracelets, or lockets. She had not the air of being about to accept an invitation to luncheon. Her dress was gray and plain, but it fitted her figure perfectly. In her neat black turban hat was the gold-green wing of a macaw. On this morning she was softly and shyly radiant. Her eyes were dreamily bright, her cheeks genuine peach-blow, her expression a happy one, tinged with memory.

Pitcher, still mildly curious, noticed a difference in her ways this morning. Instead of going straight into the adjoining room, where her desk was, she lingered in the outer office. Once she moved over by Maxwell's desk, near enough for him to be aware of her presence.

The machine sitting at that desk was no longer a man; it was a busy New York broker, moved by buzzing wheels and uncoiling springs.

"Well—what is it? Anything?" asked Maxwell, sharply. His opened mail lay like a bank of stage snow on his crowded desk. His keen gray eye flashed upon her half impatiently.

"Nothing," answered the stenographer, moving away with a little smile.

"Mr. Pitcher," she said to the confidential clerk, "did Mr. Maxwell say anything yesterday about engaging another stenographer?"

"He did," answered Pitcher. "He told me to get another one. I notified the agency yesterday afternoon to send over a few samples this morning. It's 9:45 and not a single picture hat or piece of pineapple chewing gum has showed up yet."

"I will do the work as usual, then," said the young lady, "until someone comes to fill the place." And she went to her desk at once and hung the black turban hat with the gold-green macaw wing in its accustomed place.

He who has been denied the spectacle of a busy Manhattan broker during a rush of business is handicapped for the profession of anthropology. The poet sings of the "crowded hour of glorious life." The broker's hour is not only crowded, but minutes and seconds are hanging to all the straps and packing both front and rear platforms.

And this day was Harvey Maxwell's busy day. The ticker began to reel out jerkily its coils of tape, the desk telephone had a chronic attack of buzzing. Men began to throng into the office and call at him over the railing, jovially, sharply, viciously, excitedly. Messenger boys ran in and out with messages and telegrams. The clerks in the office jumped about like sailors during a storm. Even Pitcher's face relaxed into something resembling animation.

On the Exchange[1] there were hurricanes and landslides

---

[1] The Exchange: the Stock Exchange.

and snowstorms and glaciers and volcanoes, and those elemental disturbances were reproduced in the broker's offices. Maxwell shoved his chair against the wall and transacted business after the manner of a toe dancer. He jumped from ticker to phone, from desk to door with the trained agility of a dancer.

In the midst of this growing and important stress the broker became suddenly aware of a high-rolled fringe of golden hair under a nodding canopy of velvet and ostrich tips, imitation sealskin, and a string of beads as large as hickory nuts, ending near the floor with a silver heart. There was a self-possessed young lady connected with these accessories.

"Lady from the Stenographer's Agency to see about the position," said Pitcher.

Maxwell turned half around, with his hands full of papers and ticker tape.

"What position?" he asked, with a frown.

"Position of stenographer," said Pitcher. "You told me yesterday to call them up and have one sent over this morning."

"You are losing your mind, Pitcher," said Maxwell. "Why should I have given you any such instructions? Miss Leslie has given perfect satisfaction during the year she has been here. The place is hers as long as she chooses to retain it. There's no place open here, madam. Cancel that order with the agency, Pitcher, and don't bring any more of 'em in here."

The silver heart left the office, swinging and banging itself against the office furniture as it departed. Pitcher seized a moment to remark to the bookkeeper that the "old man" seemed to get more absent-minded and forgetful every day of the world.

The rush and pace of business grew fiercer and faster. On the floor they were pounding half a dozen stocks in which Maxwell's customers were heavy investors. Orders to buy and sell were coming and going as swift as the flight of swallows. Some of his own holdings were imperiled, and the man was working like some high-geared, delicate, strong

machine—strung to full speed, accurate, never hesitating, with the proper word and decision and act ready and prompt as clockwork. Stocks and bonds, loans and mortgages, margins and securities—here was a world of finance, and there was no room in it for the human world or the world of nature.

When the luncheon hour drew near there came a slight lull in the uproar.

Maxwell stood by his desk with his hands full of telegrams and notes, with a fountain pen over his right ear and his hair ranging in disorderly strings over his forehead. His window was open, for the beloved janitress, Spring, had turned on a little warmth through the waking registers of the earth.

And through the window came a wandering—perhaps a lost—odor—a delicate, sweet odor of lilac that fixed the broker for a moment immovable. For this odor belonged to Miss Leslie; it was her own, and hers only.

The odor brought her vividly, almost tangibly before him. The world of finance dwindled suddenly to a speck. And she was in the next room—twenty steps away.

"By George, I'll do it now," said Maxwell, half aloud. "I'll ask her now. I wonder I didn't do it long ago."

He dashed into the inner office with the haste of a short trying to cover. He charged upon the desk. He still clutched fluttering papers with both hands and the pen was above his ear.

"Miss Leslie," he began, hurriedly, "I have but a moment to spare. I want to say something in that moment. Will you be my wife? I haven't had time to make love to you in the ordinary way, but I really do love you. Talk quick, please— those fellows are clubbing the stuffing out of Union Pacific."

"Oh, what are you talking about?" exclaimed the young lady. She rose to her feet and gazed upon him, round-eyed.

"Don't you understand?" said Maxwell, restively. "I want you to marry me. I love you, Miss Leslie. I wanted to tell you, and I snatched a minute when things had slackened up a bit. They're calling me for the phone now. Tell 'em to wait a minute, Pitcher. Won't you, Miss Leslie?"

The stenographer acted very queerly. At first she seemed overcome with amazement; then tears flowed from her wondering eyes; and then she smiled sunnily through them, and one of her arms slid tenderly about the broker's neck.

"I know now," she said, softly. "It's this old business that has driven everything else out of your head for the time. I was frightened at first. Don't you remember, Harvey? We were married last evening at 8 o'clock in the Little Church around the Corner."

The Ransom
of
Red Chief

The kidnappers considered themselves desperate men. After Red Chief had joined them, they realized that they hadn't even known what desperate meant.

It looked like a good thing: but wait till I tell you. We were down South, in Alabama—Bill Driscoll and myself—when this kidnapping idea struck us.

There was a town down there, as flat as a flannel-cake, and called Summit, of course. It contained inhabitants of as self-satisfied a class of peasantry as ever clustered around a Maypole.

Bill and me had a joint capital of about six hundred dollars, and we needed just two thousand dollars more to pull off a crooked town-lot scheme in Western Illinois with. We talked it over on the front steps of the hotel. Philoprogenitoveness,[1] says we, is strong in semi-rural communities; therefore, a kidnapping project ought to do better there than in the radius of newspapers that send reporters out in plain clothes to stir up talk about such things. We knew that Summit couldn't get after us with anything stronger than constables and, maybe, some bloodhounds and an article or two in the *Weekly Farmers' Budget*. So, it looked good.

We selected for our victim the only child of a prominent citizen named Ebenezer Dorset. The father was respectable

[1] Philoprogenitoveness: the love of parents for their children.

and tight, a mortgage fancier and a stern, upright collection-plate passer and forecloser. The kid was a boy of ten, with freckles, and hair the color of the cover of the magazine you buy at the newsstand when you want to catch a train. Bill and me figured that Ebenezer would melt down for a ransom of two thousand dollars to a cent. But wait till I tell you.

About two miles from Summit was a little mountain, covered with many cedar trees. On the rear elevation of this mountain was a cave. There we stored provisions.

One evening after sundown, we drove in a buggy past old Dorset's house. The kid was in the street, throwing rocks at a kitten on the opposite fence.

"Hey, little boy!" says Bill, "would you like to have a bag of candy and a nice ride?"

The boy catches Bill neatly in the eye with a piece of brick.

"That will cost the old man an extra five hundred dollars," says Bill, climbing over the wheel.

That boy put up a fight like a welter-weight cinnamon bear; but, at last, we got him down in the bottom of the buggy and drove away. We took him up to the cave, and I hitched the horse nearby. After dark I drove the buggy to the little village three miles away, where we had hired it, and walked back to the mountain.

Bill was pasting court plaster over the scratches and bruises on his features. There was a fire burning behind the big rock at the entrance of the cave, and the boy was watching a pot of boiling coffee, with two buzzard tail-feathers stuck in his red hair. He points a stick at me when I come up, and says:

"Ha! cursed paleface, do you dare to enter the camp of Red Chief, the terror of the plains?"

"He's all right now," says Bill, rolling up his trousers and examining some bruises on his shins. "We're playing Indian. We're making Buffalo Bill's show look like magic-lantern views of Palestine in the town hall. I'm Old Hank, the Trapper, Red Chief's captive, and I'm to be scalped at daybreak. By Geronimo! that kid can kick hard."

Yes, sir, that boy seemed to be having the time of his life. The fun of camping out in a cave had made him forget that he was a captive himself. He immediately christened me Snake-eye, the Spy, and announced that, when his braves returned from the warpath, I was to be broiled at the stake at the rising of the sun.

Then we had supper; and he filled his mouth full of bacon and bread and gravy, and began to talk. He made a during-dinner speech something like this:

"I like this fine. I never camped out before; but I had a pet 'possum once, and I was nine last birthday. I hate to go to school. Rats ate up sixteen of Jimmy Talbot's aunt's speckled hen's eggs. Are there any real Indians in these woods? I want some more gravy. Does the trees moving make the wind blow? We had five puppies. What makes your nose so red, Hank? My father has lots of money. Are the stars hot? I whipped Ed Walker twice, Saturday. I don't like girls. You don't catch toads unless with a string. Do oxen make any noise? Why are oranges round? Have you got beds to sleep on in this cave? Amos Murray has got six toes. A parrot can talk, but a monkey or a fish can't. How many does it take to make twelve?"

Every few minutes he would remember that he was a chief, and pick up his stick rifle and tiptoe to the mouth of the cave to look for the scouts of the hated paleface. Now and then he would let out a warwhoop that made Old Hank the Trapper shiver. That boy had Bill terrorized from the start.

"Red Chief," says I to the kid, "would you like to go home?"

"Aw, what for?" says he. "I don't have any fun at home. I hate to go to school. I like to camp out. You won't take me back home again, Snake-eye, will you?"

"Not right away," says I. "We'll stay here in the cave awhile."

"All right!" says he. "That'll be fine. I never had such fun in all my life."

We went to bed about eleven o'clock. We spread down some wide blankets and quilts and put Red Chief between us. We weren't afraid he'd run away. He kept us awake for three hours, jumping up and reaching for his rifle and screeching: "Hist! pard," in mine and Bill's ears, as the fancied crackle of a twig or the rustle of a leaf revealed to his young imagination the approach of the outlaw band. At last, I fell into a troubled sleep, and dreamed that I had been kidnapped and chained to a tree by a fierce pirate with red hair.

Just at daybreak, I was awakened by a series of awful screams from Bill. They weren't yells, or howls, or shouts, or whoops, or yawps, such as you'd expect from a manly set of vocal organs—they were simply indecent, terrifying, humiliating screams, such as women emit when they see ghosts or caterpillars. It's an awful thing to hear a strong desperate fat man scream in a cave at daybreak.

I jumped up to see what the matter was. Red Chief was sitting on Bill's chest, with one hand twined in Bill's hair. In the other he had the sharp case knife we used for slicing bacon; and he was industriously and realistically trying to take Bill's scalp, according to the sentence that had been pronounced upon him the evening before.

I got the knife away from the kid and made him lie down again. But, from that moment, Bill's spirit was broken. He laid down on his side of the bed, but he never closed an eye again in sleep as long as that boy was with us. I dozed off for a while, but along toward sunup I remembered that Red Chief had said I was to be burned at the stake at the rising of the sun. I wasn't nervous or afraid; but I sat up and lit my pipe and leaned against a rock.

"What you getting up so soon for, Sam?" asked Bill.

"Me?" says I. "Oh, I got a kind of pain in my shoulder. I thought sitting up would rest it."

"You're a liar!" says Bill. "You're afraid. You was to be burned at sunrise, and you was afraid he'd do it. And he would, too, if he could find a match. Ain't it awful, Sam? Do you think anybody will pay out money to get a little imp like that back home?"

"Sure," said I. "A rowdy kid like that is just the kind that parents dote on. Now, you and the Chief get up and cook breakfast, while I go up on the top of this mountain and look around."

I went up on the peak of the little mountain and ran my eye over the vicinity. Over toward Summit I expected to see the men of the village armed with scythes and pitchforks beating the countryside for the kidnappers. But what I saw was a peaceful landscape dotted with one man ploughing with a mule. Nobody was dragging the creek; no messengers dashed hither and yon, bringing tidings of no news to the distracted parents. "Perhaps," says I to myself, "it has not yet been discovered that the wolves have borne away the tender lambkin from the fold. Heaven help the wolves!" says I, and I went down the mountain to breakfast.

When I got to the cave I found Bill backed up against the side of it, breathing hard, and the boy threatening to smash him with a rock half as big as a coconut.

"He put a red-hot boiled potato down my back," explained Bill, "and then mashed it with his foot; and I boxed his ears. Have you got a gun about you, Sam?"

I took the rock away from the boy and kind of patched up the argument. "I'll fix you," says the kid to Bill. "No man ever yet struck the Red Chief but he got paid for it. You better beware!"

After breakfast the kid takes a piece of leather with strings wrapped around it out of his pocket and goes outside the cave unwinding it.

"What's he up to now?" says Bill, anxiously. "You don't think he'll run away, do you, Sam?"

"No fear of it," say I. "He don't seem to be much of a homebody. But we've got to fix up some plan about the ransom. There don't seem to be much excitement around Summit on account of his disappearance; but maybe they haven't realized yet that he's gone. His folks may think he's spending the night with Aunt Jane or one of the neighbors. Anyhow, he'll be missed today. Tonight we must get a message to his father demanding the two thousand dollars for his return."

Just then we heard a kind of war-whoop, such as David might have emitted when he knocked out the champion Goliath. It was a sling that Red Chief had pulled out of his pocket, and he was whirling it around his head.

I dodged, and heard a heavy thud and a kind of a sigh from Bill. A rock the size of an egg had caught Bill just behind his left ear. He loosened himself all over and fell in the fire across the frying pan of hot water for washing the dishes. I dragged him out and poured cold water on his head for half an hour.

By and by, Bill sits up and feels behind his ear and says: "Sam, do you know who my favorite Biblical character is?"

"Take it easy," says I. "You'll come to your senses presently."

"King Herod,"[2] says he. "You won't go away and leave me here alone, will you, Sam?"

I went out and caught that boy and shook him until his freckles rattled.

"If you don't behave," says I, "I'll take you straight home. Now, are you going to be good, or not?"

"I was only funning," says he, sullenly. "I didn't mean to hurt Old Hank. But what did he hit me for? I'll behave, Snake-eye, if you won't send me home, and if you'll let me play the Black Scout today."

---

[2] Herod: an ancient king who, according to the Bible, had children put to death.

"I don't know the game," says I. "That's for you and Mr. Bill to decide. He's your playmate for the day. I'm going away for a while, on business. Now, you come in and make friends with him and say you are sorry for hurting him, or home you go, at once."

I made him and Bill shake hands, and then I took Bill aside and told him I was going to Poplar Grove, a little village three miles from the cave, and find out what I could about how the kidnapping had been regarded in Summit. Also, I thought it best to send a letter to old man Dorset that day, demanding the ransom and dictating how it should be paid.

"You know, Sam," says Bill, "I've stood by you without batting an eye in earthquakes, fire, and flood—in poker games, dynamite outrages, police raids, train robberies, and cyclones. I never lost my nerve yet till we kidnapped that two-legged skyrocket of a kid. He's got me going. You won't leave me long with him, will you, Sam?"

"I'll be back some time this afternoon," says I. "You must keep the boy amused and quiet till I return. And now we'll write the letter to old Dorset."

Bill and I got paper and pencil and worked on the letter while Red Chief, with a blanket wrapped around him, strutted up and down, guarding the mouth of the cave. Bill begged me tearfully to make the ransom fifteen hundred dollars instead of two thousand. "I ain't attempting," says he, "to decry the celebrated moral aspect of parental affection, but we're dealing with humans, and it ain't human for anybody to give up two thousand dollars for that forty-pound chunk of freckled wildcat. I'm willing to take a chance at fifteen hundred dollars. You can charge the difference up to me."

So, to relieve Bill, I acceded, and we wrote a letter that ran this way:

EBENEZER DORSET, ESQ.:
We have your boy concealed in a place far from Summit.

It is useless for you or the most skillful detectives to find him. Absolutely, the only terms on which you can have him restored to you are these: We demand fifteen hundred dollars in large bills for his return; the money to be left at midnight tonight at the same spot and in the same box as your reply. If you agree to these terms, send your answer in writing by a solitary messenger tonight at half-past eight o'clock. After crossing Owl Creek on the road to Poplar Grove, there are three large trees about a hundred yards apart, close to the fence of the wheat field on the right-hand side. At the bottom of the fence-post, opposite the third tree, will be found a small pasteboard box.

The messenger will place the answer in this box and return immediately to Summit.

If you attempt any treachery or fail to comply with our demand as stated, you will never see your boy again.

If you pay the money as demanded, he will be returned to you safe and well within three hours. These terms are final, and if you do not agree to them no further communication will be attempted.

TWO DESPERATE MEN

I addressed this letter to Dorset, and put it in my pocket. As I was about to start, the kid comes up to me and says:

"Aw, Snake-eye, you said I could play the Black Scout while you was gone."

"Play it, of course," says I. "Mr. Bill will play with you. What kind of a game is it?"

"I'm the Black Scout," says Red Chief, "and I have to ride to the stockade to warn the settlers that the Indians are coming. I'm tired of playing Indian myself. I want to be the Black Scout."

"All right," says I. "It sounds harmless to me. I guess Mr. Bill will help you."

"What am I to do?" asks Bill, looking at the kid suspiciously.

"You are the hoss," says Black Scout. "Get down on

your hands and knees. How can I ride to the stockade without a hoss?"

"You'd better keep him interested," said I, "till we get the scheme going. Loosen up."

Bill gets down on his all fours, and a look comes in his eye like a rabbit's when you catch it in a trap.

"How far is it to the stockade, kid?" he asks, in a husky manner of voice.

"Ninety miles," says the Black Scout. "And you have to gallop to get there on time. Whoa, now!"

The Black Scout jumps on Bill's back and digs his heels in his side.

"For Heaven's sake," says Bill, "Hurry back, Sam, as soon you can. I wish we hadn't made the ransom more than a thousand. Say, you quit kicking me or I'll get up and warm you good."

I walked over to Poplar Grove and sat around the post-office and store, talking with the chaw-bacons that came in to trade. One old man says that he hears Summit is all upset on account of Elder Ebenezer Dorset's boy having been lost or stolen. That was all I wanted to know. I bought some smoking tobacco, referred casually to the price of black-eyed peas, posted my letter and came away. The postmaster said the mail carrier would come by in an hour to take the mail to Summit.

When I got back to the cave Bill and the boy were not to be found. I explored the vicinity of the cave, and risked a yodel or two, but there was no response.

So I lighted my pipe and sat down on a mossy bank to await developments.

In about half an hour I heard the bushes rustle, and Bill wobbled out into the little glade in front of the cave. Behind him was the kid, stepping softly like a scout, with a broad grin on his face. Bill stopped, took off his hat, and wiped his face with a red handkerchief. The kid stopped about eight feet behind him.

"Sam," says Bill, "I suppose you'll think I'm a traitor, but I couldn't help it. The boy is gone. I sent him home. All is off. There was martyrs in old times," goes on Bill, "that suffered death rather than give up the particular graft they enjoyed. None of 'em ever was tortured as I have been. I tried to be faithful, but there came a limit."

"What's the trouble, Bill?" I asks him.

"I was rode," says Bill, "the ninety miles to the stockade, not barring an inch. Then, when the settlers was rescued, I was given oats. And then, for an hour I had to try to explain to him why there was nothin' in holes, how a road can run both ways, and what makes the grass green. I tell you, Sam, a human can only stand so much. I takes him by the neck of his clothes and drags him down the mountain. On the way he kicks my legs black and blue from the knees down; and I've got to have two or three bites on my thumb and hand cauterized.

"But he's gone"—continues Bill—"gone home. I showed him the road to Summit and kicked him about eight feet nearer there at one kick. I'm sorry we lose the ransom; but it was either that or Bill Driscoll to the madhouse."

Bill is puffing and blowing, but there is a look of peace and growing content on his rose-pink features.

"Bill," says I, "there isn't any heart disease in your family, is there?"

"No," says Bill, "nothing chronic except malaria and accidents. Why?"

"Then you might turn around," says I, "and have a look behind you."

Bill turns and sees the boy, and loses his complexion and sits down plump on the ground and begins to pluck aimlessly at grass and little sticks. For an hour I was afraid of his mind. And then I told him that my scheme was to put the whole job through immediately and that we would get the ransom and be off with it by midnight if Old Dorset fell in with our proposition.

I had a scheme for collecting that ransom without danger of being caught. The tree under which the answer was to be left—and the money later on—was close to the road fence with big, bare fields on all sides. If a gang of constables should be watching for anyone to come for the note, they could see him a long way off crossing the fields or in the road. But no, sirree! At half-past eight I was up in that tree as well hidden as a tree toad, waiting for the messenger to arrive.

Exactly on time, a half-grown boy rides up the road on a bicycle, locates the pasteboard box at the foot of the fence-post, slips a folded piece of paper into it, and pedals away again back toward Summit.

I waited an hour and then concluded the thing was square. I slid down the tree, got the note, slipped along the fence till I struck the woods, and was back at the cave in another half an hour. I opened the note, got near the lantern, and read it to Bill. It was written with a pen in a crabbed hand, and the sum and substance of it was this:

TWO DESPERATE MEN

Gentlemen: I received your letter today by post, in regard to the ransom you ask for the return of my son. I think you are a little high in your demands, and I hereby make you a counter-proposition, which I believe you will accept. You bring Johnny home and pay me two hundred and fifty dollars in cash and I agree to take him off your hands. You had better come at night, for the neighbors believe he is lost, and I couldn't be responsible for what they would do to anybody they saw bringing him back. Very respectfully,

EBENEZER DORSET

"Great pirates of Penzance," says I; "of all the impudent—"
But I glanced at Bill, and hesitated. He had the most

appealing look in his eyes I ever saw on the face of a dumb or a talking brute.

"Sam," says he, "what's two hundred and fifty dollars, after all? We've got the money. One more night of this kid will send me to a bed in Bedlam[3]. You ain't going to let the chance go, are you?"

"Tell you the truth, Bill," says I, "this little monster has somewhat got on my nerves too. We'll take him home, pay the ransom, and make our getaway."

We took him home that night. We got him to go by telling him that his father had bought a silver-mounted rifle and a pair of moccasins for him, and we were to hunt bears the next day.

It was just twelve o'clock when we knocked at Ebenezer's front door. Just at the moment when I should have been taking the fifteen hundred dollars from the box under the tree, according to the original proposition, Bill was counting out two hundred and fifty dollars into Dorset's hand.

When the kid found out we were going to leave him at home he started to howl and fastened himself as tight as a leech to Bill's leg. His father peeled him away gradually, like a porous plaster.

"How long can you hold him?" asks Bill.

"I'm not as strong as I used to be," says old Dorset, "but I think I can promise you ten minutes."

"Enough," says Bill. "In ten minutes I shall cross the Central, Southern, and Middle Western States, and be heading for the Canadian border."

And, as dark as it was, and as fat as Bill was, and as good a runner as I am, he was a good mile and a half out of Summit before I could catch up with him.

---

[3] Bedlam: a madhouse.

After Twenty Years

Both Bob and Jim were on hand to keep their date made such a long time before—but a lot can happen in twenty years.

The policeman on the beat moved up the avenue slowly. The time was barely 10 o'clock at night, but chilly gusts of wind with a tase of rain in them had well nigh emptied the streets.

Trying doors as he went, twirling his club with many intricate and artful movements, turning now and then to cast his watchful eye down the street, the officer, with his stalwart form and slight swagger, made a fine picture of a guardian of the peace. The vicinity was one that kept early hours. Now and then you might see the lights of a cigar store or of an all-night lunch counter; but the majority of the doors belonged to business places that had long since been closed.

When about midway of a certain block, the policeman suddenly slowed his walk. In the doorway of a darkened hardware store a man leaned, with an unlighted cigar in his mouth. As the policeman walked up to him the man spoke up quickly.

"It's all right, officer," he said calmly. "I'm just waiting for a friend. It's an appointment made twenty years ago. Sounds a little funny to you, doesn't it? Well, I'll explain if you'd like to make certain it's all straight. About that long ago there used to be a restaurant where this store stands—'Big Joe' Brady's restaurant."

"Until five years ago," said the policeman. "It was torn down then."

The man in the doorway struck a match and lit his cigar. The light showed a pale, square-jawed face with keen eyes, and a little white scar near his right eyebrow. His scarfpin was a large diamond, oddly set.

"Twenty years ago tonight," said the man, "I dined here at 'Big Joe' Brady's with Jimmy Wells, my best chum, and the finest chap in the world. He and I were raised here in New York, just like two brothers, together. I was eighteen and Jimmy was twenty. The next morning I was to start for the West to make my fortune. You couldn't have dragged Jimmy out of New York. He thought it was the only place on earth. Well, we agreed that night that we would meet here again exactly twenty years from that date and time, no matter what our conditions might be or from what distance we might have to come. We figured that in twenty years each of us ought to have our destiny worked out and our fortunes made, whatever they were going to be."

"It sounds pretty interesting," said the policeman. "Rather a long time between meets, though, it seems to me. Haven't you heard from your friend since you left?"

"Well, yes, for a time we corresponded," said the other. "But after a year or two we lost track of each other. You see, the West is a pretty big proposition, and I kept hustling around over it pretty lively. But I know Jimmy will meet me here if he's alive, for he always was the truest, staunchest old chap in the world. He'll never forget. I came a thousand miles to stand in this door tonight, and it's worth it if my old partner turns up."

The waiting man pulled out a handsome watch, the lids of it set with small diamonds.

"Three minutes to ten," he announced. "It was exactly ten o'clock when we parted here at the restaurant door."

"Did pretty well out West, didn't you?" asked the policeman.

"You bet! I hope Jimmy has done half as well. He was a kind of a plodder, though, good fellow as he was. I've had to compete with some of the sharpest wits going to get my pile. A man gets in a groove in New York. It takes the West to put a razor-edge on him."

The policeman twirled his club and took a step or two.

"I'll be on my way. Hope your friend comes around all right. Going to call time on him sharp?"

"I should say not!" said the other. "I'll give him half an hour at least. If Jimmy is alive on earth he'll be here by that time. So long, officer."

"Good-night, sir," said the policeman, passing on along his beat, trying doors as he went.

There was now a fine, cold drizzle falling, and the wind had risen from its uncertain puffs into a steady blow. The few foot passengers astir in that quarter hurried dismally and silently along with coat collars turned high and pocketed hands. And in the door of the hardware store the man who had come a thousand miles to fill an appointment with the friend of his youth, smoked his cigar and waited.

About twenty minutes he waited, and then a tall man in a long overcoat, with collar turned up to his ears, hurried across from the opposite side of the street. He went directly to the waiting man.

"Is that you, Bob?" he asked, doubtfully.

"Is that you, Jimmy Wells?" cried the man in the door.

"Bless my heart!" exclaimed the new arrival, grasping both the other's hands with his own. "It's Bob, sure as fate. I was certain I'd find you here if you were still in existence. Well, well, well!—twenty years is a long time. The old restaurant's gone, Bob; I wish it had lasted, so we could have had another dinner there. How has the West treated you, old man?"

"Bully; it has given me everything I asked it for. You've

changed lots, Jimmy. I never thought you were so tall by two or three inches."

"Oh, I grew a bit after I was twenty."

"Doing well in New York, Jimmy?"

"Moderately. I have a position in one of the city departments. Come on, Bob; we'll go around to a place I know of, and have a good long talk about old times."

The two started up the street, arm in arm. The man from the West was beginning to outline the history of his career. The other listened with interest.

At the corner stood a drugstore, brilliant with electric lights. When they came into this glare each of them turned to gaze upon the other's face.

The man from the West stopped suddenly and released his arm.

"You're not Jimmy Wells," he snapped. "Twenty years is a long time, but not long enough to change a man's nose from a Roman to a pug."

"It sometimes changes a good man into a bad one," said the tall man. "You've been under arrest for ten minutes, 'Silky' Bob. Chicago thinks you may have dropped over our way and wires us it wants to have a chat with you. Going quietly, are you? That's sensible. Now, before we go to the station here's a note I was asked to hand to you. You may read it here at the window. It's from Patrolman Wells."

The man from the West unfolded the little piece of paper handed him. His hand was steady when he began to read, but it trembled a little by the time he had finished. The note was rather short.

Bob: I was at the appointed place on time. When you struck the match to light your cigar I saw it was the face of the man wanted in Chicago. Somehow I couldn't do it myself, so I went around and got a plain-clothes man to do the job.

JIMMY

The Furnished Room

It was a shabby mean little place, this room, which held within its four walls a very important secret.

Restless, shifting, fugacious[1] as time itself is a certain vask bulk of the population of the red brick district of the lower West Side. Homeless, they have a hundred homes. They flit from furnished room to furnished room, transients forever—transients in abode, transients in heart, and mind. They sing "Home, Sweet Home" in ragtime; they carry their *lares et penates*[2] in a bandbox; their vine is entwined about a picture hat; a rubber plant is their fig tree.

Hence the houses of this district, having had a thousand dwellers, should have a thousand tales to tell, mostly dull ones, no doubt; but it would be strange if there could not be found a ghost or two in the wake of all these vagrant guests.

One evening after dark a young man prowled among these crumbling red mansions, ringing their bells. At the twelfth he rested his bag upon the step and wiped the dust from his hatband and forehead. The bell sounded faint and far away in some remote, hollow depths.

To the door of this, the twelfth house whose bell he had rung, came a housekeeper who made him think of an un-

[1] Fugacious: fleeting, soon vanishing.

[2] Lares et penates: the guardian spirits of the hearth and home in Roman mythology.

wholesome worm that had eaten its nut to a hollow shell and now sought to fill the vacancy with edible lodgers.

He asked if there was a room to let.

"Come in," said the housekeeper. Her voice came from her throat; her throat seemed lined with fur. "I have the third-floor back, vacant since a week back. Should you wish to look at it?"

The young man followed her up the stairs. A faint light from no particular source eased the shadows of the halls. They trod noiselessly upon a worn stair carpet. At each turn of the stairs were vacant niches in the wall. Perhaps plants had once been set within them. If so they had died in that foul and tainted air. It may be that statues of the saints had stood there, but it was not difficult to conceive that imps and devils had dragged them forth in the darkness and down to the unholy depth of some furnished pit below.

"This is the room," said the housekeeper, from her furry throat. "It's a nice room. It ain't often vacant. I had some most elegant people in it last summer—no trouble at all, and paid in advance to the minute. The water's at the end of the hall. Sprowls and Mooney kept it three months. They done a vaudeville sketch. Miss B'retta Sprowls—you may have heard of her—Oh, that was just the stage names—right there over the dresser is where the marriage certificate hung, framed. The gas is here, and you see there is plenty of closet room. It's a room everybody likes. It never stays idle long."

"Do you have many theatrical people rooming here?" asked the young man.

"They comes and goes. A good proportion of my lodgers is connected with the theaters. Yes, sir, this is the theatrical district. Actor people never stays long anywhere. I get my share. Yes, they comes and they goes."

He engaged the room, paying for a week in advance. He was tired, he said, and would take possession at once. He counted out the money. The room had been made ready, she said, even to towels and water. As the housekeeper moved away he put, for the thousandth time, the question that he carried at the end of his tongue.

"A young girl—Miss Vashner—Miss Eloise Vashner—do you remember such a one among your lodgers? She would be singing on the stage, most likely. A fair girl, of medium height and slender, with reddish, gold hair and a dark mole near her left eyebrow."

"No, I don't remember the name. Them stage people has names they change as often as their rooms. They comes and they goes. No, I don't call that one to mind."

No. Always no. Five months of ceaseless questions and the inevitable negative. So much time spent by day in questioning managers, agents, schools, and choruses; by night among the audiences of theaters from all-star casts down to music halls so low that he dreaded to find her. He was sure that since her disappearance from home this great, water-girt city held her somewhere.

The furnished room received its latest guest with a false smile. The sophistical comfort came in reflected gleams from the decayed furniture, the ragged brocade upholstery of a couch and two chairs, a foot-wide cheap pier glass between the two windows, from one or two gilt picture frames and a brass bedstead in a corner.

One by one, the little signs left by the furnished room's procession of guests developed a significance. The threadbare space in the rug in front of the dresser told that a lovely woman had marched in the throng. The tiny fingerprints on the wall spoke of little prisoners trying to feel their way to sun and air. A splattered stain, raying like the shadow of a bursting bomb, witnessed where a hurled glass or bottle had splintered with its contents against the wall. Across the pier glass had been scrawled with a diamond in staggering letters the name "Marie." It seemed that the succession of dwellers in the furnished room had turned in fury—and wreaked upon it their passions. The furniture was chipped and bruised; the couch, distorted by bursting springs, seemed a horrible monster that had been slain during the stress of some great struggle. Some more potent upheaval had cloven a great slice from the marble mantel. Each plank in the floor owned its particular squeak as from a separate and individual agony. It seemed incredible that all this malice and injury had been wrought upon the room by those who had called it for a time their home; and yet it may have been the cheated home instinct surviving blindly, the resentful rage at false household gods that had kindled their anger. A hut that is our own we can sweep and adorn and cherish.

The young tenant allowed these thoughts to file, softshod, through his mind, while there drifted into the room furnished sounds and furnished scents. He heard in one room a tittering and immoderate, slack laughter; in others the monologue of a scold, the rattling of dice, a lullaby, and one crying dully; above him a banjo tinkled with spirit. Doors banged somewhere; the elevated trains roared intermittently; a cat yowled miserably upon a back fence. And he breathed the breath of the house—a dank savor rather than a smell— a cold, musty stench as from underground vaults mingled with the reeking exhalations of linoleum and mildewed and rotten woodwork.

Then suddenly, as he rested there, the room was filled with the strong, sweet odor of mignonette. It came as upon a single buffet of wind with such sureness and fragrance and emphasis that it almost seemed a living visitant. And the man cried aloud: "What, dear?" as if he had been called, and sprang up and faced about. The rich odor clung to him and wrapped him around. He reached out his arms for it, all his senses for the time confused and commingled. How could one be called by an odor? Surely it must have been a sound. But, was it not the sound that had touched, that had caressed him?

"She has been in this room," he cried, and he sprang to wrest from it a token, for he knew he would recognize the smallest thing that had belonged to her or that she had touched. This enveloping scent of mignonette, the odor that she had loved and made her own—whence came it?

The room had been but carelessly set in order. Scattered upon the flimsy dresser scarf were half a dozen hairpins—those discreet, indistinguishable friends of womankind, feminine of gender, infinite of mood, and uncommunicative of tense. These he ignored, conscious of their triumphant lack of identity. Ransacking the drawers of the dresser he came upon a discarded, tiny, ragged handkerchief. He pressed it to his face. It smelled of heliotrope; he hurled it to the floor. In another drawer he found odd buttons, a theater programme, a pawnbroker's card, two lost marshmallows, a book on dreams. In the last was a woman's black satin hair bow, which halted him, poised between ice and fire. But the black satin hair bow also is femininity's demure, impersonal common ornament and tells no tales.

And then he traversed the room like a hound on the scent, skimming the walls, considering the corners of the bulging matting on his hands and knees, rummaging mantel and tables, the curtains and hangings, the drunken cabinet in the corner, for a visible sign, unable to perceive that she was there beside, around, against, within, above him, clinging to him, wooing him, calling him so tenderly through the finer senses that even his grosser ones became aware of the call. Once again he answered loudly: "Yes, dear!" and turned, wild-eyed, to gaze on vacancy, for he could not yet discern form and color and love and outstretched arms in the odor of mignonette. Oh, God! whence that odor, and since when have odors had a voice to call? Thus he groped.

He burrowed in crevices and corners, and found corks and cigarettes. These he passed in passive contempt. But once he found in a fold of the matting a half-smoked cigar, and this he ground beneath his heel. He sifted the room from end to end. He found dreary and ignoble small records of many a tenant; but of her whom he sought, and who may have lodged

there, and whose spirit seemed to hover there, he found no trace.

And then he thought of the housekeeper.

He ran from the haunted room downstairs and to a door that showed a crack of light. She came out to his knock. He smothered his excitement as best he could.

"Will you tell me, madam," he besought her, "who occupied the room I have before I came?"

"Yes, sir. I can tell you again. 'Twas Sprowls and Mooney,

as I said. Miss B'retta Sprowls it was in the theaters, but Missis Mooney she was. My house is well known for respectability. The marriage certificate hung, framed, on a nail over—"

"What kind of a lady was Miss Sprowls—in looks, I mean?"

"Why, black-haired, sir, short, and stout, with a comical face. They left a week ago Tuesday."

"And before they occupied it?"

"Why, there was a single gentleman connected with the draying business. He left owing me a week. Before him was Missis Crowder and her two children, that stayed four months; and back of them was old Mr. Doyle, whose sons paid for him. He kept the room six months. That goes back a year, sir, and further I do not remember."

He thanked her and crept back to his room. The room was dead. The perfume of mignonette had departed. In its place was the old, stale odor of moldy house furniture, of atmosphere in storage.

The ebbing of his hope drained his faith. He sat staring at the yellow, singing gaslight. Soon he walked to the bed and began to tear the sheets into strips. With the blade of his knife he drove them tightly into every crevice around windows and door. When all was snug and taut he turned out the light, turned the gas full on again and laid himself gratefully upon the bed.

It was Mrs. McCool's night to go with the can for beer. So she fetched it and sat with Mrs. Purdy in the basement.

"I rented out my third-floor-back this evening," said Mrs. Purdy, across a fine circle of foam. "A young man took it. He went up to bed two hours ago."

"Now, did ye, Mrs. Purdy, ma'am?" said Mrs. McCool, with intense admiration. "You do be a wonder for rentin' rooms of that kind. And did ye tell him, then?" she concluded in a husky whisper laden with mystery.

"Rooms," said Mrs. Purdy, in her furriest tones, "are furnished for to rent. I did not tell him, Mrs. McCool."

69

"'Tis right ye are, ma'am; 'tis by renting rooms we kape alive. Ye have the rale sense for business, ma'am. There be many people will rayjict the rentin' of a room if they be tould a suicide has been after dyin' in the bed of it."

"As you say, we has our living to be making," remarked Mrs. Purdy.

"Yis, ma'am; 'tis true. 'Tis just one wake ago this day I helped ye lay out the third-floor-back. A pretty slip of a collen she was to be killin' herself wid the gas—a swate little face she had, Mrs. Purdy, ma'am."

"She'd a-been called handsome, as you say," said Mrs. Purdy, assenting but critical, "but for that mole she had a-growin' by her left eyebrow. Do fill your glass again, Mrs. McCool."

A Retrieved Reformation

To Jimmy Valentine a kit of burglar's tools had once meant a blown safe, a quick get-away, and then some easy money before the police caught up with him. But one day he found a far different use for it.

A guard came to the prison shoe-shop, where Jimmy Valentine was stitching uppers, and escorted him to the front office. There the warden handed Jimmy his pardon, which had been signed that morning by the governor. Jimmy took it in a tired kind of way. He had served nearly ten months of a four-year sentence. He had expected to stay only about three months, at the longest. When a man with as many friends on the outside as Jimmy Valentine had is received in the "stir" it is hardly worthwhile to cut his hair.

"Now, Valentine," said the warden, "you'll go out in the morning. Brace up, and make a man of yourself. You're not a bad fellow at heart. Stop cracking safes, and live straight."

"Me?" said Jimmy, in surprise. "Why, I never cracked a safe in my life."

"Oh, no," laughed the warden. "Of course not. Let's see, now. How was it you happened to get sent up on that Springfield job? Was it because you wouldn't prove an alibi for fear of compromising somebody in extremely high-toned society? Or was it simply a case of a mean old jury that had it in for you? It's always one or the other with you innocent victims."

"Me?" said Jimmy, still blankly virtuous. "Why, warden, I never was in Springfield in my life!"

"Take him back, Cronin," smiled the warden, "and fix him up with outgoing clothes. Unlock him in the morning, and let him come to the bull pen. Better think over my advice, Valentine."

At a quarter past seven on the next morning Jimmy stood in the warden's outer office. He had on a suit of the ill fitting, ready-made clothes and a pair of the stiff, squeaky shoes that the state furnishes to its discharged compulsory guests.

The clerk handed him a railroad ticket and the five-dollar bill with which the law expected him to rehabilitate himself into good citizenship and prosperity. The warden gave him a cigar, and shook hands. Valentine, 9762, was chronicled on the books "Pardoned by Governor," and Mr. James Valentine walked out into the sunshine.

Disregarding the song of the birds, the waving green trees, and the smell of the flowers, Jimmy headed straight for a restaurant. There he tasted the first sweet joys of liberty in the shape of a broiled chicken and a bottle of white wine—followed by a cigar a grade better than the one the warden had given him. From there he proceeded leisurely to the depot. He tossed a quarter into the hat of a blind man sitting by the door, and boarded his train. Three hours set him down in a little town near the state line. He went to the café of one Mike Dolan and shook hands with Mike, who was alone behind the bar.

"Sorry we couldn't make it sooner, Jimmy, me boy," said Mike. "But we had the protest from Springfield to buck against, and the governor nearly refused. Feeling all right?"

"Fine," said Jimmy. "Got my key?"

He got his key and went upstairs, unlocking the door of a room at the rear. Everything was just as he had left it. There on the floor was Ben Price's collar-button that had been torn from that eminent detective's shirtband when they had overpowered Jimmy to arrest him.

Pulling out from the wall a folding bed, Jimmy slid back a panel in the wall and dragged out a dust-covered suitcase. He opened this and gazed fondly at the finest set of burglar's tools in the East. It was a complete set, made of specially tempered steel, the latest designs in drills, punches, braces and bits, jimmies, clamps, and augers, with two or three novelties invented by Jimmy himself, in which he took pride. Over nine hundred dollars they had cost him.

In half an hour Jimmy went downstairs and through the café. He was now dressed in tasteful and well-fitting clothes, and carried his dusted and cleaned suitcase in his hand.

"Got anything on?" asked Mike Dolan, genially.

"Me?" said Jimmy, in a puzzled tone. "I don't understand. I'm representing the New York Amalgamated Short Snap Biscuit Cracker and Frazzled Wheat Company."

This statement delighted Mike to such an extent that Jimmy had to take a seltzer-and-milk on the spot. He never touched "hard" drinks.

A week after the release of Valentine, 9762, there was a neat job of safe-burglary done in Richmond, Indiana, with no clue to the author. A scant eight hundred dollars was all that was secured. Two weeks after that a patented, improved, burglarproof safe in Logansport was opened to the tune of fifteen hundred dollars, currency. Securities and silver were untouched. That began to interest the rogue catchers. Then an old-fashioned bank-safe in Jefferson City became active and threw out of its crater an eruption of bank notes amounting to five thousand dollars. The losses were now high enough to bring the matter up into Ben Price's class of work. By comparing notes, a remarkable similarity in the methods of the burglaries was noticed. Ben Price investigated the scenes of the robberies, and was heard to remark:

"That's Dandy Jim Valentine's autograph. He's resumed

business. Look at that combination knob—jerked out as easy as pulling up a radish in wet weather. He's got the only clamps that can do it. And look how clean those tumblers were punched out! Jimmy never has to drill but one hole. Yes, I guess I want Mr. Valentine. He'll do his bit next time without any short-time or clemency foolishness."

Ben Price knew Jimmy's habits. He had learned them while working up the Springfield case. Long jumps, quick getaways, no confederates, and a taste for good society—these ways had helped Mr. Valentine to become noted as a successful dodger of retribution. It was given out that Ben Price had taken up the trail of the elusive cracksman, and other people with burglarproof safes felt more at ease.

One afternoon Jimmy Valentine and his suitcase climbed out of the mail hack in Elmore, a little town five miles off the railroad down in the blackjack country of Arkansas. Jimmy, looking like an athletic young senior just home from college, went down the board sidewalk toward the hotel.

A young lady crossed the street, passed him at the corner and entered a door over which was the sign "The Elmore Bank." Jimmy Valentine looked into her eyes, forgot what he was, and became another man. She lowered her eyes and colored slightly. Young men of Jimmy's style and looks were scarce in Elmore.

Jimmy collared a boy who was loafing on the steps of the bank as if he were one of the stockholders, and began to ask him questions about the town, feeding him dimes at intervals. By and by the young lady came out, looking royally unconscious of the young man with the suitcase, and went her way.

"Isn't that young lady Miss Polly Simpson?" asked Jimmy.

"Naw," said the boy. "She's Annabel Adams. Her pa owns this bank. What'd you come to Elmore for? Is that a gold watch-chain? I'm going to get a bulldog. Got any more dimes?"

Jimmy went to the Planters' Hotel, registered as Ralph

D. Spencer, and engaged a room. He said he had come to Elmore to look for a location to go into business. How was the shoe business, now, in the town? He had thought of the shoe business. Was there an opening?

The clerk was impressed by the clothes and manner of Jimmy. He, himself, was something of a pattern of fashion to the youth of Elmore, but he now perceived his short-comings. While trying to figure out Jimmy's manner of tying his four-in-hand he cordially gave information.

Yes, there ought to be a good opening in the shoe line. There wasn't an exclusive shoe store in the place. The dry-goods and general stores handled them. Business in all lines was fairly good. Hoped Mr. Spencer would decide to locate in Elmore. He would find it a pleasant town to live in, and the people very sociable.

Mr. Spencer thought he would stop over in the town a few days and look over the situation. No, the clerk needn't call the boy. He would carry up his suitcase, himself; it was rather heavy.

Mr. Ralph Spencer remained in Elmore, and prospered. He opened a shoe store and secured a good run of trade.

Socially he was also a success, and made many friends. And he accomplished the wish of his heart. He met Miss Annabel Adams, and became more and more captivated by her charms.

At the end of a year the situation of Mr. Ralph Spencer was this: he had won the respect of the community, his shoe store was flourishing, and he and Annabel were engaged to be married in two weeks. Mr. Adams, the typical, plod-ding, country banker, approved of Spencer. Annabel's pride in him almost equaled her affection. He was as much at home in the family of Mr. Adams and that of Annabel's married sister as if he were already a member.

One day Jimmy sat down in his room and wrote this letter, which he mailed to the safe address of one of his friends in St. Louis:

Dear Old Pal:

I want you to be at Sullivan's place, next Wednesday night at nine o'clock. I want you to wind up some little matters for me. And, also, I want to make you a present of my kit of tools. I know you'll be glad to get them—you couldn't duplicate the lot for a thousand dollars. Say, Billy, I've quit the old business—a year ago. I've got a nice store. I'm making an honest living, and I'm going to marry the finest girl on earth two weeks from now. It's the only life, Billy—the straight one. I wouldn't touch a dollar of another man's money now for a million. After I get married I'm going to sell out and go West, where there won't be so much danger of having old scores brought up against me. I tell you, Billy, she's an angel. She believes in me; and I wouldn't do another crooked thing for the whole world. Be sure to be at Sully's, for I must see you. I'll bring along the tools with me.

Your old friend,
Jimmy

On the Monday night after Jimmy wrote this letter, Ben Price jogged into Elmore in a livery buggy. He lounged about town in his quiet way until he found out what he wanted to know. From the drugstore across the street from Spencer's shoe store he got a good look at Ralph D. Spencer.

"Going to marry the banker's daughter are you, Jimmy?" said Ben to himself, softly. "Well, I don't know!"

The next morning Jimmy took breakfast at the Adamses. He was going to Little Rock that day to order his wedding suit and buy something nice for Annabel. That would be the first time he had left town since he came to Elmore. It had been more than a year now since those last professional "jobs," and he thought he could safely venture out.

After breakfast quite a family party went down town together—Mr. Adams, Annabel, Jimmy, and Annabel's married sister with her two little girls, aged five and nine. They came by the hotel where Jimmy still boarded, and he ran up to his room and brought along his suitcase. Then they went on to the bank. There stood Jimmy's horse and buggy and Dolph Gibson, who was going to drive him over to the railroad station.

All went inside the high, carved oak railings into the banking room—Jimmy included, for Mr. Adams's future son-in-law was welcome anywhere. The clerks were pleased to be greeted by the good-looking, agreeable young man who was going to marry Miss Annabel. Jimmy set his suitcase down. Annabel, whose heart was bubbling with happiness and lively youth, put on Jimmy's hat and picked up the suitcase. "Wouldn't I make a nice drummer?" said Annabel. "My! Ralph, how heavy it is. Feels like it was full of gold bricks."

"Lot of nickel-plated shoe-horns in there," said Jimmy, coolly, "that I'm going to return. Thought I'd save express charges by taking them up. I'm getting awfully economical."

The Elmore Bank had just put in a new safe and vault. Mr. Adams was very proud of it, and insisted on an inspection by everyone. The vault was a small one, but it had a new patented door. It fastened with three solid steel bolts thrown at the same time with a single handle, and had a time-lock. Mr. Adams beamingly explained its workings to Mr. Spencer, who showed a courteous but not too intelligent interest. The two children, May and Agatha, were delighted by the shining metal and funny clock and knobs.

While they were thus engaged Ben Price sauntered in and leaned on his elbow, looking casually inside between the railings. He told the teller that he didn't want anything; he was just waiting for a man he knew.

Suddenly there was a scream or two from the women, and a commotion. May, the nine-year-old girl, in a spirit of play, had shut Agatha in the vault. She had then shot the bolts and turned the knob of the combination as she had seen Mr. Adams do.

The old banker sprang to the handle and tugged at it for a

moment. "The door can't be opened," he groaned. "The clock hasn't been wound nor the combination set."

Agatha's mother screamed again, hysterically.

"Hush!" said Mr. Adams, raising his trembling hand. "All be quiet for a moment. Agatha!" he called as loudly as he could. "Listen to me." During the following silence they could just hear the faint sound of the child wildly shrieking in the dark vault in a panic of terror.

"My precious darling!" wailed the mother. "She will die of fright! Open the door! Oh, break it open! Can't you men do something?"

"There isn't a man nearer than Little Rock who can open that door," said Mr. Adams, in a shaky voice. "My God! Spencer, what shall we do? That child—she can't stand it long in there. There isn't enough air, and, besides, she'll go into convulsions from fright."

Agatha's mother, frantic now, beat the door of the vault with her hands. Somebody wildly suggested dynamite. Annabel turned to Jimmy, her large eyes full of anguish, but not yet despairing. To a woman nothing seems quite impossible to the powers of the man she worships.

"Can't you do something, Ralph—try, won't you?"

He looked at her with a queer, soft smile on his lips and in his keen eyes.

"Annabel," he said, "give me that rose you are wearing, will you?"

Hardly believing that she heard him aright, she unpinned the bud from the bosom of her dress, and placed it in his hand. Jimmy stuffed it into his vestpocket, threw off his coat and pulled up his shirtsleeves. With that act Ralph D. Spencer passed away and Jimmy Valentine took his place.

"Get away from the door, all of you," he commanded, shortly.

He set his suitcase on the table, and opened it out flat. From that time on he seemed to be unconscious of anyone else. He laid out the shining tools swiftly and orderly, whis-

tling softly to himself as he always did when at work. In a deep silence and immovable, the others watched him as if under a spell.

In a minute Jimmy's pet drill was biting smoothly into the steel door. In ten minutes—breaking his own record— he threw back the bolts and opened the door.

Agatha, almost collapsed, but safe, was gathered into her mother's arms.

Jimmy Valentine put on his coat, and walked outside the railings toward the front door. As he went he thought he heard a far-away voice that he once knew call "Ralph!" But he never hesitated.

At the door a big man stood somewhat in his way.

"Hello, Ben!" said Jimmy, still with his strange smile. "Got around at last, have you? Well, let's go. I don't know that it makes much difference now."

And then Ben Price acted rather strangely.

"Guess you're mistaken, Mr. Spencer," he said. "Don't believe I recognize you. Your buggy's waiting for you, ain't it?"

And Ben Price turned and strolled down the street.

The Third Ingredient

Hetty had the meat and Cecilia had the potatoes. It takes one more ingredient to make a good stew, though!

The (so-called) Vallambrosa Apartment House is not an apartment house. It is composed of two old-fashioned, brownstone-front residences welded into one. The parlor floor of one side is gay with the wraps and headgear of a dress shop. The other is frightening with the grisly display of a painless dentist. You may have a room there for two dollars a week or you may have one for twenty dollars. Among the Valambrosa's roomers are stenographers, musicians, brokers, shopgirls, art students, and other people who lean far over the banister-rail when the door-bell rings.

At six o'clock one afternoon Hetty Pepper came back to her third-floor rear $3.50 room in the Vallambrosa with her nose and chin more sharply pointed than usual. To be discharged from the department store where you have been working four years, and with only fifteen cents in your purse, does have a tendency to make your features appear more finely chiselled.

And now for Hetty's thumb-nail biography while she climbs the two flights of stairs.

She walked into the Biggest Store one morning four years before, with seventy-five other girls, applying for a job behind the waist department counter. They formed a bewildering scene of beauty, carrying a total mass of blond hair sufficient to have justified the horseback gallops of a hundred Lady Godivas[1].

The capable, cool-eyed, impersonal, young, bald-headed man, whose task it was to engage six of the contestants, was aware of a feeling of suffocation as if he were drowning while white clouds, hand-embroidered, floated about him. And then a sail hovered in sight. Hetty Pepper, homely of countenance, with small, green eyes and chocolate-colored hair, dressed in a suit of plain burlap and a common-sense hat, stood before him with every one of her twenty-nine years of life unmistakably in sight.

"You're on!" shouted the bald-headed young man, and was saved. And that is how Hetty came to be employed in the Biggest Store. The story of her rise to an eight-dollar-a-week salary is the combined stories of Hercules, Joan of Arc, Una, Job, and Little-Red-Riding-Hood. You shall not learn from me the salary that was paid her as a beginner. There is a sentiment growing about such things, and I want no millionaire store-proprietors climbing the fire-escape of my tenement house to throw dynamite bombs into my skylight.

The story of Hetty's discharge from the Biggest Store is so nearly a repetition of her engagement as to be monotonous.

In each department of the store there is a person carrying always a mileage book and a red necktie, and referred to as a "buyer." The destinies of the girls in his department who live on so much per week are in his hands.

This particular buyer was a capable, cool-eyed, impersonal, young, bald-headed man. As he walked along the aisles of his department he seemed to be sailing while white clouds, machine-embroided, floated around him. He looked upon Hetty Pepper's homely countenance, emerald eyes, and chocolate-colored hair as a welcome oasis of green in a desert of beauty. In a quiet angle of a counter he pinched her arm

[1] Lady Godiva: according to an old English legend, she rode through the streets of Coventry naked to fulfill the terms of a wager.

kindly, three inches above the elbow. She slapped him three feet away with one good blow of her muscular and not especially lily-white right. So, now you know why Hetty Pepper came to leave the Biggest Store at thirty minutes' notice, with one dime and a nickel in her purse.

This morning's quotations list the price of rib beef at six cents per (butcher's) pound. But on the day that Hetty was "released" by the B.S. the price was seven and one half cents. That fact is what makes this story possible. Otherwise, the extra four cents would have—

Hetty mounted with her rib beef to her $3.50 third-floor-back. One hot, savory beef-stew for supper, a night's good sleep, and she would be fit in the morning to apply again for the tasks of Hercules, Joan of Arc, Una, Job, and Little-Red-Riding-Hood.

In her room she got the graniteware stew-pan out of the 2 X 4 foot china—er—I mean earthenware closet and began to dig down in a rat's-nest of paper bags for the potatoes and onions. She came out with her nose and chin just a little sharper pointed.

There was neither a potato nor an onion. Now, what kind of a beefstew can you make out of simply beef? You can make oyster-soup without oysters, turtle-soup without turtles, coffee-cake without coffee, but you can't make beef-stew without potatoes and onions.

But rib beef alone, in an emergency, can make an ordinary pine door look like a wrought-iron gambling house portal to the wolf. With salt and pepper and a tablespoonful of flour (first well stirred in a little cold water) 'twill serve—'tis not so deep as a lobster à la Newburgh, nor so wide as a church festival doughnut; but 'twill serve.

Hetty took her stewpan to the rear of the third-floor hall. According to the advertisements of the Vallambrosa there was running water to be found there. Between you and me and the water meter, it only ambled or walked through the faucets, but technicalities have no place here. There was also a sink where housekeeping roomers often met to dump their coffee grounds and glare at one another's kimonos.

At this sink Hetty found a girl with heavy, gold-brown, artistic hair and plaintive eyes washing two large "Irish" potatoes. Hetty knew the Vallambrosa as well as anyone. The kimonos were her encyclopedia, her "Who's What?" her clearing-house of news, of goers and comers. From a rose-pink kimono edged with Nile green she had learned that the girl with the potatoes was a miniature-painter living in a kind of attic—or "studio," as they prefer to call it—on the top floor. Hetty was not certain in her mind what a miniature was; but it certainly wasn't a house; because house-painters, although they wear splashy overalls and poke ladders in your face on the street, are known to indulge in a riotous profusion of food at home.

The potato girl was quite slim and small, and handled her potatoes as an old bachelor uncle handles a baby who is cutting teeth. She had a dull shoemaker's knife in her right hand, and she had begun to peel one of the potatoes with it.

"Beg pardon," Hetty said, "for butting into what's not my business, but if you peel them potatoes you lose out. They're new Bermudas. You want to scrape 'em. Lemme show you."

She took a potato and the knife, and began to demonstrate.

"Oh, thank you," breathed the artist. "I didn't know. And I *did* hate to see the thick peeling go; it seemed such a waste. But I thought they always had to be peeled. When you've got only potatoes to eat, the peelings count, you know."

"Say, kid," said Hetty, staying her knife, "you ain't up against it, too, are you?"

The miniature artist smiled starvedly.

"I suppose I am. Art—or, at least, the way I interpret it—doesn't seem to be much in demand. I have only these potatoes for my dinner. But they aren't so bad boiled and hot, with a little butter and salt."

"Child," said Hetty, letting a brief smile soften her rigid

features, "Fate has sent me and you together. I've had it handed to me in the neck, too; but I've got a chunk of meat in my room as big as a lapdog. And I've done everything to get potatoes except pray for 'em. Let's me and you bunch our goods and make a stew of 'em. We'll cook it in my room. If we only had an onion to go in it! Say, kid, you haven't got a couple of pennies that've slipped down into the lining of your last winter's sealskin, have you? I could step down to the corner and get one at old Giuseppe's stand. A stew without an onion is worse'n a matinée without candy."

"You may call me Cecilia," said the artist. "No; I spent my last penny three days ago."

"Then we'll have to cut the onion out instead of slicing it in," said Hetty. "I'd ask the janitress for one, but I don't want 'em hep just yet to the fact that I'm pounding the asphalt for another job. But I wish we did have an onion."

In the shop-girl's room the two began to prepare their supper. Cecilia's part was to sit on the couch helplessly and beg to be allowed to do something, in the voice of a cooing ring-dove. Hetty prepared the rib beef, putting it in cold salted water in the stew-pan and setting it on the one-burner gas-stove.

"I wish we had an onion," said Hetty, as she scraped the two potatoes.

On the wall opposite the couch was pinned a flaming gorgeous advertising picture of one of the new ferryboats of the P.U.F.F. Railroad that had been built to cut down the time between Los Angeles and New York City one-eighth of a minute.

Hetty, turning her head during her continuous monologue, saw tears running from her guest's eyes as she gazed on the picture of the speeding, foam-girdled transport.

"Why, say, Cecilia, kid," said Hetty, poising her knife, "is it as bad art as that? I ain't a critic, but I thought it kind of brightened up the room. Of course, a manicure-painter could tell it was a bum picture in a minute. I'll take it down if you say so. I wish to the holy Saint Potluck we had an onion."

But the miniature miniature-painter had tumbled down, sobbing, with her nose indenting the hard-woven drapery of the couch.

Hetty knew. She had accepted her role long ago. How scant the words with which we try to describe a single quality of a human being! When we reach the abstract we are lost. The nearer to Nature that the babbling of our lips comes, the better do we understand. Figuratively (let us say), some people are Bosoms, some are Hands, some are Heads, some are Muscles, some are Feet, some are Backs for burdens.

Hetty was a Shoulder. Hers was a sharp, sinewy shoulder; but all her life people had laid their heads upon it, and had left there all or half their toubles. Looking at Life anatomically, which is as good a way as any, she was chosen to be a Shoulder. There were few truer collarbones anywhere than hers.

Hetty was only thirty-three, and she had not yet outlived the little pang that visited her whenever the head of youth and beauty leaned upon her for consolation. But one glance in her mirror always served as an instantaneous painkiller. So she gave one pale look into the crinkly old looking-glass on the wall above the gas stove, turned down the flame a little lower from the bubbling beef and potatoes, went over to the couch, and lifted Cecilia's head.

"Go on and tell me, honey," she said. "I know now that it ain't art that's worrying you. You met him on a ferry-boat, didn't you? Go on, Cecilia, kid, and tell your—your Aunt Hetty about it."

But youth and melancholy must first spend the surplus of sighs and tears that waft and float the bark of romance to its harbor in the delectable isles. Presently, Cecilia told her story without art or illumination.

"It was only three days ago. I was coming back on the ferry from Jersey City. Old Mr. Schrum, an art dealer, told me of a rich man in Newark who wanted a miniature of his daughter painted. I went to see him and showed him some of my work. When I told him the price would be fifty dollars he laughed at me like a hyena. He said an enlarged crayon twenty times the size would cost him only eight dollars.

"I had just enough money to buy my ferry ticket back to New York. I felt as if I didn't want to live another day. I must have looked as I felt, for I saw *him* on the row of seats opposite me, looking at me as if he understood. He was nice looking, but, oh, above everything else, he looked kind. When one is tired or unhappy or hopeless, kindness counts more than anything else.

"When I got so miserable that I couldn't fight against it any longer, I got up and walked slowly out the rear door of the ferryboat cabin. No one was there, and I slipped quickly over the rail, and dropped into the water. Oh, friend Hetty, it was cold, cold!

"For just one moment I wished I was back in the old Val-

lambrosa, starving and hoping. And then I got numb, and didn't care. And then I felt that somebody else was in the water close by me, holding me up. He had followed me, and jumped in to save me.

"Somebody threw a thing like a big, white doughnut at us, and he made me put my arms through the hole. Then the ferryboat backed up and they pulled us on board. Oh, Hetty, I was so ashamed of my wickedness in trying to drown myself; and, besides, my hair had all tumbled down and was sopping wet, and I was such a sight.

"And then some men in blue clothes came around. *He* gave them his card, and I heard him tell them he had seen me drop my purse on the edge of the boat outside the rail, and in leaning over to get it I had fallen overboard. And then I remembered having read in the papers that people who try to kill themselves are locked up in cells with people who try to kill other people, and I was afraid.

"But some ladies on the boat took me downstairs and got me nearly dry and did up my hair. When the boat landed, *he* came and put me in a cab. He was all dripping himself, but laughed as if he thought it was all a joke. He begged me, but I wouldn't tell him my name nor where I lived, I was so ashamed."

"You were a fool, child," said Hetty, kindly. "Wait till I turn the light up a bit. I wish to Heaven we had an onion."

"Then he raised his hat," went on Cecilia, "and said: 'Very well, but I'll find you, anyhow. I'm going to claim my rights of salvage.' Then he gave money to the cab-driver and told him to take me where I wanted to go, and walked away. What is 'salvage,' Hetty?"

"The edge of a piece of goods that ain't hemmed," said the shopgirl. "You must have looked pretty well frazzled out to the little hero boy."

"It's been three days," moaned the miniature-painter, "and he hasn't found me yet."

"Extend the time," said Hetty. "This is a big town. Think

of how many girls he might have to see soaked in water with their hair down before he would recognize you. The stew's getting on fine—but, oh, for an onion! I'd even use a piece of garlic if I had it."

The beef and potatoes bubbled merrily, exhaling a mouth-watering savor that yet lacked something, leaving a hunger on the palate, a haunting, wishful desire for some lost and needful ingredient.

"I came near drowning in that awful river," said Cecilia, shuddering.

"It ought to have more water in it," said Hetty; "the stew, I mean. I'll go get some at the sink."

"It smells good," said the artist.

"That nasty old North River?" objected Hetty. "It smells to me like soap factories and wet dogs—oh, you mean the stew. Well, I wish we had an onion for it. Did he look like he had money?"

"First he looked kind," said Cecilia. "I'm sure he was rich; but that matters so little. When he drew out his bill-folder to pay the cabman you couldn't help seeing hundreds and thousands of dollars in it. And I looked over the cab doors and saw him leave the ferry station in a motor-car; and the chauffeur gave him his bearskin to put on, for he was sopping wet. And it was only three days ago."

"What a fool!" said Hetty, shortly.

"Oh, the chauffeur wasn't wet," breathed Cecilia. "And he drove the car away very nicely."

"I mean *you*," said Hetty. "For not giving him your address."

"I never give my address to chauffeurs," said Cecilia haughtily.

"I wish we had one," said Hetty, disconsolately.

"What for?"

"For the stew, of course—Oh, I mean an onion."

Hetty took a pitcher and started to the sink at the end of the hall.

A young man came down the stairs from above just as she was opposite the lower step. He was decently dressed, but pale and haggard. His eyes were dull with the stress of some burden of physical or mental woe. In his hand he bore an onion—a pink, smooth, solid, shining onion, as large around as a ninety-eight-cent alarm clock.

Hetty stopped. So did the young man. There was something Joan of Arc-ish, Herculean, and Una-ish in the look and pose of the shoplady—she had cast off the roles of Job and Little-Red-Riding-Hood. The young man stopped at the foot of the stairs and coughed distractedly. He felt marooned, held up, attacked, assailed, sacked, pan-handled, browbeaten, though he knew not why. It was the look in Hetty's eyes that did it. In them he saw the Jolly Roger fly to the masthead and an able seaman with a knife between his teeth scurry up the ratlines and nail it there. But as yet he did not know that the cargo he carried was the thing that had caused him to be so nearly blown out of the water without even a parley.

"*Beg* your pardon," said Hetty, as sweetly as her dilute acetic acid tones permitted, "but did you find that onion on the stairs? There was a hole in the paper bag; and I've just come out to look for it."

The young man coughed for half a minute. The interval may have given him the courage to defend his own property. Also, he clutched his pungent prize greedily, and, with a show of spirit, faced his grim waylayer.

"No," he said, huskily. "I didn't find it on the stairs. It was given to me by Jack Bevens, on the top floor. If you don't believe it, ask him. I'll wait until you do."

"I know about Bevens," said Hetty, sourly. "He writes books and things up there. Say—do you live in the Vallambrosa?"

"I do not," said the young man. "I come to see Bevens sometimes. He's my friend. I live two blocks west."

"What are you going to do with the onion?—*begging* your pardon," said Hetty.

"I'm going to eat it."

"Raw?"

"Yes: as soon as I get home."

"Haven't you got anything else to eat with it?"

The young man considered briefly.

"No" he confessed; "there's not another scrap of anything in my diggings to eat. I think old Jack is pretty hard up for grub in his shack, too. He hated to give up the onion, but I worried him into parting with it."

"Man," said Hetty, fixing him with her all-knowing eyes, and laying a bony but impressive finger on his sleeve, "you've known trouble, too, haven't you?"

"Lots," said the onion owner, promptly. "But this onion is my own property, honestly come by. If you will excuse me, I must be going."

"Listen," said Hetty, paling a little with anxiety. "Raw onion is a mighty poor diet. And so is a beefstew without one. Now, if you're Jack Bevens's friend, I guess you're nearly right. There's a little lady—a friend of mine—in my room there at the end of the hall. Both of us are out of luck; and we had just potatoes and meat between us. They're stewing now. But it ain't got any soul. There's something lacking to it. There's certain things in life that are naturally intended to fit and belong together. One is pink cheesecloth and green roses, and one is ham and eggs, and one is Irish and trouble. And the other one is beef and potatoes *with* onions. And still another one is people who are up against it and other people in the same fix."

The young man went into a protracted fit of coughing. With one hand he hugged his onion to his bosom.

"No doubt; no doubt," said he, at length. "But, as I said, I must be going because—"

Hetty clutched his sleeve firmly.

"Don't eat raw onions. Chip in toward the dinner and line yourself inside with the best stew you ever licked a spoon over. Must two ladies knock a young gentleman down and drag him inside for the honor of dining with 'em? No harm shall befall you, Little Brother. Loosen up and fall into line."

The young man's pale face relaxed into a grin.

"Believe I'll go you," he said, brightening. "If my onion is as good as a credential, I'll accept the invitation gladly."

"It's as good as that, but better as seasoning," said Hetty. "You come and stand outside the door till I ask my lady friend if she has any objections. And don't run away with that letter of recommendation before I come out."

Hetty went into her room and closed the door. The young man waited outside.

"Cecilia, kid," said the shopgirl, oiling the sharp saw of her voice as well as she could, "there's an onion outside. With a young man attached. I've asked him in to dinner. You ain't going to kick, are you?"

"Oh, dear!" said Cecilia, sitting up and patting her artistic hair. She cast a mournful glance at the ferryboat poster on the wall.

"Nit," said Hetty. "It ain't him. You're up against real life now. I believe you said your hero friend had money and automobiles. This is a poor skeeziks that's got nothing to eat but an onion. But he's easy-spoken and not a freshy. I imagine he's been a gentleman, he's so low down now. And we need the onion. Shall I bring him in? I'll guarantee his behavior."

"Hetty, dear," sighed Cecilia, "I'm so hungry. What difference does it make whether he's a prince or a burglar? I don't care. Bring him in if he's got anything to eat with him."

Hetty went back into the hall. The onion man was gone. Her heart missed a beat, and a gray look settled over her face except on her nose and cheekbones. And then the tides of life flowed in again, for she saw him leaning out of the front window at the other end of the hall. She hurried there.

He was shouting to someone below. The noise of the street overpowered the sound of her footsteps. She looked down over his shoulder, saw whom he was speaking to, and heard his words. He pulled himself in from the window-sill and saw her standing over him.

Hetty's eyes bored into him like two steel knives.

"Don't lie to me," she said, calmly. "What were you going to do with that onion?"

The young man suppressed a cough and faced her resolutely. His manner was that of one who had been scolded enough.

"I was going to eat it," said he, with emphatic slowness; "just as I told you before."

"And you have nothing else to eat at home?"

"Not a thing."

"What kind of work do you do?"

"I am not working at anything just now."

"Then why," said Hetty, with her voice set on its sharpest edge, "do you lean out of a window and give orders to chauffeurs in green automobiles in the street below?"

The young man flushed and his dull eyes began to sparkle.

"Because, madam," said he, "I pay the chauffeur's wage and I own the automobile—and also this onion—this onion, madam."

He flourished the onion within an inch of Hetty's nose. The shoplady did not retreat a hair's-breadth.

"Then why do you eat onions," she said, with biting contempt, "and nothing else?"

"I never said I did," retorted the young man, heatedly. "I said I had nothing else to eat where I live. I am not a delicatessen storekeeper."

"Then why," pursued Hetty, inflexibly, "were you going to eat a raw onion?"

"My mother," said the young man, "always made me eat one for a cold. Pardon my referring to a physical infirmity; but you may have noticed that I have a very, very severe cold. I was going to eat the onion and go to bed. I wonder why I am standing here and apologizing to you for it."

"How did you catch this cold?" went on Hetty, suspiciously.

The young man seemed to have arrived at some extreme height of feeling. There were two choices—a burst of rage or a surrender to the ridiculous. He chose wisely; and the empty hall echoed his hoarse laughter.

"You're a dandy," said he. "And I don't blame you for being careful. I don't mind telling you. I got wet. I was on a North River ferry a few days ago when a girl jumped overboard. Of course, I—"

Hetty extended her hand, interrupting his story.

"Give me the onion," she said.

The young man set his jaw a trifle harder.

"Give me the onion," she repeated.

He grinned, and laid it in her hand.

Then Hetty's infrequent, grim, melancholy smile showed itself. She took the young man's arm and pointed with her other hand to the door of her room.

"Little Brother," she said, "go in there. The little fool you fished out of the river is there waiting for you. Go on in. I'll give you three minutes before I come. Potatoes is in there, waiting. Go on in, Onions."

After he had tapped at the door and entered, Hetty began to peel and wash the onion at the sink. She gave a gray look at the gray roofs outside and the smile on her face vanished by little jerks and twitches.

"But it's us," she said, grimly, to herself, "it's *us* that furnishes the beef."

The Clarion Call

*When a murderer and a detective pit their wits against each
other, something exciting is bound to result.*

Half of this story can be found in the records of the police
department; the other half belongs behind the business
counter of a newspaper office.

One afternoon two weeks after Millionaire Norcross was
found in his apartment murdered by a burglar, the murderer,
while strolling serenely down Broadway, ran plump against
Detective Barney Woods.

"Is that you, Johnny Kernan?" asked Woods.

"No less," cried Kernan, heartily. "If it isn't Barney
Woods, late and early of old Saint Jo! You'll have to show
me! What are you doing East? Do the green-goods circulars
get out that far?"

"I've been in New York some years," said Woods. "I'm
on the city detective force."

"Well, well!" said Kernan, breathing smiling joy and patting the detective's arm.

"Come into Muller's," said Woods, "and let's hunt a quiet
table. I'd like to talk to you awhile."

It lacked a few minutes to the hour of four. The tides
of trade were not yet loosed, and they found a quiet corner
of the café. Kernan, well dressed, slightly swaggering, self-
confident, seated himself opposite the little detective, with
his squinting eyes, and ready-made suit.

"What business are you in now?" asked Woods. "You
know you left Saint Jo a year before I did."

"I'm selling shares in a copper mine," said Kernan. "I may establish an office here. Well, well! and so old Barney is a New York detective. You always had a turn that way. You were on the police in Saint Jo after I left there, weren't you?"

"Six months," said Woods. "And now there's one more question, Johnny. I've followed your record pretty close ever since you did that hotel job in Saratoga, and I never knew you to use your gun before. Why did you kill Norcross?"

Kernan stared for a few moments with concentrated attention at the slice of lemon in his high-ball; and then he looked at the detective with a sudden crooked, brilliant smile.

"How did you guess it, Barney?" he asked, admiringly. "I swear I thought the job was as clean and as smooth as a peeled onion. Did I have a string hanging out anywhere?"

Woods laid upon the table a small gold pencil.

"It's the one I gave you the last Christmas we were in Saint Jo. I've got your shaving mug yet. I found this under a corner of the rug in Norcross's room. I warn you to be careful what you say. I've got it put on to you, Johnny. We were old friends once, but I must do my duty. You'll have to go to the chair for Norcross."

Kernan laughed.

"My luck stays with me," said he. "Who'd have thought old Barney was on my trail!" He slipped one hand inside his coat. In an instant Woods had a revolver against his side.

"Put it away," said Kernan, wrinkling his nose. "I'm only investigating. Aha! It takes nine tailors to make a man, but one can do a man up. There's a hole in that vest pocket. I took that pencil off my chain and slipped it in there in case of a scrap. Put up your gun, Barney, and I'll tell you why I had to shoot Norcross. The old fool started down the hall after me, popping at the button on the back of my coat with a peevish little .22 and I had to stop him. The old lady was

a darling. She just lay in bed and saw her $12,000 diamond necklace go without a chirp, while she begged like a panhandler to have back a little thin gold ring with a garnet worth about $3. I guess she married old Norcross for his money, all right. Don't they hang onto little trinkets from the Man Who Lost Out, though? There were six rings, two brooches and a watch. Fifteen thousand would cover the lot."

"I warned you not to talk," said Woods.

"Oh, that's all right," said Kernan. "The stuff is in my suit case at the hotel. And now I'll tell you why I'm talking. Because it's safe. I'm talking to a man I know. You owe me a thousand dollars, Barney Woods, and even if you wanted to arrest me your hand wouldn't make the move."

"I haven't forgotten," said Woods. "You counted out twenty fifties without a word. I'll pay it back some day. That thousand saved me and—well they were piling my furniture out on the sidewalk when I got back to the house."

"And so," continued Kernan, "you being Barney Woods, born as true as steel, and bound to play a man's game, can't lift a finger to arrest the man you're indebted to. Oh, I have to study men as well as Yale locks and window fastenings in my business. Now, keep quiet while I ring for the waiter. I've had a thirst for a year to two that worries me a little. If I'm ever caught the lucky sleuth will have to divide honors with the old boy Booze. But I never drink during business hours. After a job I can crook elbows with my old friend Barney with a clear conscience. What are you taking?"

The waiter came with the little decanters and the siphon and left them alone again.

"You've called the turn," said Woods, as he rolled the little gold pencil about with a thoughtful forefinger. "I've got to pass you up. I can't lay a hand on you. If I'd a-paid that money back—but I didn't, and that settles it. It's a bad break I'm making, Johnny, but I can't dodge it. You helped me once, and it calls for the same."

"I knew it," said Kernan, raising his glass, with a flushed smile of self-appreciation. "I can judge men. Here's to Barney, for 'he's a jolly good fellow.'"

"I don't believe," went on Woods quietly, as if he were thinking aloud, "that if accounts had been square between you and me, all the money in all the banks in New York could have bought you out of my hands tonight."

"I know it couldn't," said Kernan. "That's why I knew I was safe with you."

"Most people," continued the detective, "look sideways at my business. They don't class it among the fine arts and the professions. But I've always taken a kind of fool pride in it. And here is where I go 'busted.' I guess I'm a man first and a detective afterward. I've got to let you go, and then I've got to resign from the force. I guess I can drive an express wagon. Your thousand dollars is further off than ever, Johnny."

"Oh, you're welcome to it," said Kernan, with a lordly air. "I'd be willing to call the debt off, but I know you wouldn't have it. It was a lucky day for me when you borrowed it. And now, let's drop the subject. I'm off to the West on a morning train. I know a place out there where I can negotiate the Norcross sparks. Drink up, Barney, and forget your trouble. We'll have a jolly time while the police are knocking their heads together over the case. I've got one of my Sahara thirsts on tonight. But I'm in the hands—the unofficial hands—of my old friend Barney, and I won't even dream of a cop."

And then, as Kernan kept the waiter working, his weak point—a tremendous vanity and egotism began to show itself. He told story after story of his successful plunderings ingenious plots, and wicked crimes until Woods, with all his familiarity with evildoers, felt growing within him a cold hatred of the utterly vicious man who had once been his benefactor.

"I'm disposed of, of course," said Woods, at length. "But I advise you to keep under cover for a spell. The newspapers may take up this Norcross affair. There has been an epidemic of burglaries and murder in town this summer."

The word sent Kernan into a high glow of sullen and vindictive rage.

"To h—l with the newspapers," he growled. "What do they spell but brag and blow and boodle in boxcar letters? Suppose they do take up a case—what does it amount to? The police are easy enough to fool; but what do the newspapers do? They send a lot of pinhead reporters around to the scene; and they make for the nearest saloon and have beer while they take photos of the bartender's oldest daughter in evening dress to print as the fiancée of the young man on the tenth floor, who thought he heard a noise below on the night of the murder. That's about as near as the newspapers ever come to running down Mr. Burglar."

"Well, I don't know," said Woods, reflecting. "Some of the papers have done good work in that line. There's the *Morning Mars,* for instance. It warmed up two or three trails, and got the man after the police had let 'em get cold."

"I'll show you," said Kernan, rising and expanding his chest. "I'll show you what I think of newspapers in general, and your *Morning Mars* in particular."

Three feet from their table was the telephone booth. Kernan went inside and sat down, leaving the door open. He found a number in the book, took down the receiver, and made his demand upon Central. Woods sat still, looking at the sneering, cold face waiting close to the transmitter, and listened to the words that came from the thin lips curved into a smile.

"That the *Morning Mars?* . . . I want to speak to the managing editor. . . . Why, tell him it's someone who wants to talk to him about the Norcross murder.

"You the editor? . . . All right. . . . I am the man who killed old Norcross. . . . Wait! Hold the wire. I'm not the usual crank . . . Oh, there isn't the slightest danger. I've just been discussing it with a detective friend of mine. I killed the old man at 2:30 A.M. two weeks ago tomorrow. . . . Have a drink with you? Now, hadn't you better leave that kind of talk to your funny man? Can't you tell whether a man's lying to you or whether you're being offered the biggest scoop your dull dishrag of a paper ever had? . . . Well, that's so. It's a bobtail scoop—but you can hardly expect me to phone in my name and address. . . . Why! Oh, because I heard you make a specialty of solving mysterious crimes that stump the police. . . . No, that's not all. I want to tell you that your rotten, lying penny sheet is of no more use in tracking an intelligent murderer or highwayman than a blind poodle would be. . . . What? . . . Oh, no, this isn't a rival newspaper office. You're getting it straight. I did the Norcross job, and I've got the jewels in my suitcase at—'the name of the hotel could not be learned'—you recognize that phrase, don't you? I thought so. You've used it often enough. Kind of rattles you, doesn't it, to have the mysterious villain call up your great, big, all-powerful organ of right and justice and good government and tell you what a helpless old gas-bag you are? . . . Cut that out. You're not that big a fool—no, you don't think I'm a fraud. I can tell it by your voice. . . . Now, listen, and I'll give you a pointer that will prove it to you. Of course you've had this murder case worked over by your staff of bright young blockheads. Half of the second button on old Mrs. Norcross's night gown is broken off. I saw it when I took the garnet ring off her finger. I thought it was a ruby. . . . Stop that! It won't work."

Kernan turned to Woods with a diabolic smile.

"I've got him going. He believes me now. He didn't quite cover the transmitter with his hand when he told somebody to call up Central on another phone and get our number. I'll give him just one more dig and then we'll make a 'get-away.'

"Hello! . . . Yes, I'm here yet. You didn't think I'd run from such a little subsidized, turncoat rag of newspaper, did you? . . . Have me inside of forty-eight hours? Say, will you quit being funny? Now, you let grown men alone and attend to your business of hunting up divorce cases and street-car accidents and printing the filth and scandal that you make your living by. Good-by, old boy—sorry I haven't time to call on you. Tra-la!"

"He's as mad as a cat that's lost a mouse," said Kernan, hanging up the receiver and coming out. "And now, Barney, my boy, we'll go to a show and enjoy ourselves until a reasonable bedtime. Four hours' sleep for me, and then the west-bound."

The two dined in a Broadway restaurant. Kernan was pleased with himself. He spent money like a prince of fiction. And then a weird and gorgeous musical comedy engaged their attention. Afterward there was a late supper in a grill-room, with champagne, and Kernan at the height of his complacency.

Half-past three in the morning found them in a corner of an all-night café, Kernan still boasting in a rambling way, Woods thinking moodily over the end that had come to his usefulness as an upholder of the law.

But, as he pondered, his eye brightened.

"I wonder if it's possible," he said to himself, "I wonder if it's pos-si-ble!"

And then outside the café the comparative stillness of the early morning was punctured by faint, uncertain cries that seemed mere fireflies of sound, some growing louder, some fainter, waxing and waning amid the rumble of mild wagons and infrequent cars. Shrill cries they were when near—well-known cries that conveyed many meanings to the ears of those of the slumbering millions of the great city who waked to hear them. Cries that bore upon their significant, small volume the weight of a world's woe and laughter and delight and stress. To some, cowering beneath the protection of a night's cover, they brought news of the hideous, bright day. To others wrapped in happy sleep, they announced a morning that would dawn blacker than sable night. To many of the rich they brought a broom to sweep away what had been theirs while the stars shone. To the poor they brought—another day.

All over the city the cries were starting up, heralding the chances that the slipping of one cogwheel in the machinery of time had made; giving to the sleepers while they lay at the mercy of fate, the vengeance, profit, grief, reward, and doom that the new day had brought them. Shrill and yet plaintive were the cries, as if the young voices grieved that so much evil and so little good was in their hands. Thus echoed in the streets of the helpless city the transmission of the latest decrees of the gods, the cries of the newsboys—the Clarion Call of the Press.

Woods flipped a dime to the waiter, and said:

"Get me a *Morning Mars*."

When the paper came he glanced at its first page, and then tore a leaf out of his note book and began to write on it with the little gold pencil.

"What's the news?" yawned Kernan.

Woods flipped over to him the piece of writing:

The New York *Morning Mars:*

Please pay to the order of John Kernan the one thousand dollars reward coming to me for his arrest and conviction.

Barnard Woods

"I kind of thought they would do that," said Woods, "when you were jollying 'em so hard. Now, Johnny, you'll come to the police station with me."

Schools
and
Schools

When one of the sides of a love triangle is a smart little gal from the West like Nevada Warren, you never can tell what will happen. You can be pretty sure she'll get her man, though.

Old Jerome Warren lived in a hundred-thousand-dollar house at 35 East Fifty-Soforth Street. He was a downtown broker, so rich that he could afford to walk—for his health—a few blocks in the direction of his office every morning and then call a cab.

He had an adopted son, the son of an old friend named Gilbert who was becoming a successful painter as fast as he could squeeze the paint out of his tubes. Another member of the household was Barbara Ross, a step-niece. Man is born to trouble; so, as old Jerome had no family of his own, he took up the burdens of others.

Gilbert and Barbara got along swimmingly. There was an understanding all round that the two would stand up under a floral bell some high noon, and promise the minister to keep old Jerome's money in a state of high commotion. But at this point complication must be introduced.

Thirty years before, when old Jerome was young Jerome, there was a brother of his named Dick. Dick went West to seek his or somebody else's fortune. Nothing was heard of him until one day old Jerome had a letter from his brother. It was badly written on ruled paper that smelled of salt bacon and coffee-grounds.

It appeared that instead of Dick having forced Fortune to stand and deliver, he had been held up himself, and made to give hostages to the enemy. That is, as his letter disclosed, he was on the point of pegging out with a collection of disorders that even whiskey had failed to check. All that his 30 years of prospecting had netted him was one daughter, 19 years old, as per invoice, whom he was shipping East, charges prepaid, for Jerome to clothe, feed, educate, comfort, and cherish for the rest of her natural life or until matrimony should them part.

Old Jerome was a board-walk. Everybody knows that the world is supported by the shoulders of Atlas; and that Atlas stands on a railfence; and that the railfence is built on a turtle's back. Now, the turtle has to stand on something; and that is a board-walk made of men like old Jerome.

They met Nevada Warren at the station. She was a little girl, deeply sunburned, and wholesomely good-looking, with a manner that was frankly unsophisticated. Looking at her, somehow you would expect to see her in a short skirt and leather leggings, shooting glass balls or taming wild horses. But in her plain white blouse and black skirt she sent you guessing again. With an easy show of strength she swung along a heavy valise, which the uniformed porters tried in vain to wrest from her.

"I am sure we shall be the best of friends," said Barbara, pecking at the firm, sunburned cheek.

"I hope so," said Nevada.

"Dear little niece," said old Jerome, "you are as welcome to my house as if it were your father's own."

"Thanks," said Nevada.

"And I am going to call you 'cousin,'" said Gilbert, with his charming smile.

"Take the valise, please," said Nevada. "It weighs a million pounds. It's got samples from six of dad's old mines in it," she explained to Barbara. "I calculate they'd assay about nine cents to the thousand tons, but I promised him to bring them along."

II

It is a common custom to refer to the usual complications between one man and two ladies as the triangle. But they are never unqualified triangles. They are always isosceles—never equilateral. So, upon the coming of Nevada Warren, she and Gilbert and Barbara Ross lined up into such a figurative triangle. And of that triangle Barbara formed the hypotenuse.

One morning old Jerome was lingering long after breakfast over the dullest morning paper in the city before setting forth to his downtown fly-trap. He had become quite fond of Nevada, finding in her much of his dead brother's quiet independence and unsuspicious frankness.

A maid brought in a note for Miss Nevada Warren.

"A messenger delivered it at the door, please," she said. "He's waiting for an answer."

Nevada, who was whistling a Spanish waltz between her teeth, and watching the carriages and autos roll by in the street, took the envelope. She knew it was from Gilbert, before she opened it, by the little gold palette in the upper left-hand corner.

After tearing it open she pored over the contents for a while, absorbedly. Then, with a serious face, she went and stood at her uncle's elbow.

"Uncle Jerome, Gilbert is a nice boy, isn't he?"

"Why, bless the child!" said old Jerome, crackling his paper loudly; "of course he is. I raised him myself."

"He wouldn't write anything to anybody that wasn't exactly—I mean that everybody couldn't know and read, would he?"

"I'd just like to see him try it," said uncle, tearing a hand-ful from his newspaper. "Why, what—"

106

"Read this note he just sent me, uncle, and see if you think it's all right and proper. You see, I don't know much about city people and their ways."

Old Jerome threw his paper down and set both his feet upon it. He took Gilbert's note and fiercely read it twice, and then a third time.

"Why, child," said he, "you had me almost excited, although I was sure of that boy. He's a copy of his father, and he was a gilt edged diamond. He only asks if you and Barbara will be ready at four o'clock this afternoon for an automobile drive over to Long Island. I don't see anything to criticize in it except the stationery. I always did hate that shade of blue."

"Would it be all right to go?" asked Nevada, eagerly.

"Yes, yes, yes, child, of course. Why not? Still, it pleases me to see you so careful and candid. Go, by all means."

"I didn't know," said Nevada, demurely. "I thought I'd ask you. Couldn't you go with us, uncle?"

"I? No, no, no, no! I've ridden once in a car that boy was driving. Never again! But it's entirely proper for you and Barbara to go. Yes, yes. But I will not. No, no, no, no!"

Nevada flew to the door, and said to the maid:

"You bet we'll go. I'll answer for Miss Barbara. Tell the boy to say to Mr. Warren, 'You bet we'll go.'"

"Nevada," called old Jerome, "pardon me, my dear, but wouldn't it be as well to send him a note in reply? Just a line would do."

"No, I won't bother about that," said Nevada, gayly. "Gilbert will understand—he always does. I never rode in an automobile in my life; but I've paddled a canoe down Little Devil River through the Lost Horse Canyon, and if it's any livelier than that I'd like to know!"

III

Two months are supposed to have elapsed.

Barbara sat in the study of the hundred-thousand-dollar

house. It was a good place for her. Many places are provided in the world where men and women may repair for the purpose of getting themselves out of difficulties. There are cloisters, wailing-places, watering-places, confessionals, hermitages, lawyers' offices, beauty-parlors, airships, and studies. The greatest of these are studies.

It usually takes a hypotenuse a long time to discover that it is the longest side of a triangle. But it's a long line that has no turning.

Barbara was alone. Uncle Jerome and Nevada had gone to the theater. Barbara had not cared to go. She wanted to stay at home and study in the study. If you, miss, were a stunning New York girl, and saw every day that a suntanned Western witch was getting hobbles and a lasso on the young man you wanted for yourself, you, too, would lose taste for the silver setting of a musical comedy.

Barbara sat by the library table. Her right arm rested upon the table, and her fingers nervously manipulated a sealed letter. The letter was addressed to Nevada Warren; and in the upper left-hand corner of the envelope was Gilbert's little gold palette. It had been delivered at nine o'clock, after Nevada had left.

Barbara would have given her pearl necklace to know what that letter contained. She could not open and read it by the aid of steam, or a pen-handle, or a hair-pin, or any of the generally approved methods because her position in society forbade such an act. She had tried to read some of the lines of the letter by holding the envelope up to a strong light and pressing it hard against the paper, but Gilbert had too good a taste in stationery to make that possible.

At eleven-thirty the theater-goers returned. It was a delicious winter night. Even so far as from the cab to the door they were powdered thickly with the big flakes downpouring diagonally from the east. Old Jerome growled good-naturedly about villainous cab service and blockaded streets. Nevada, colored like a rose, with sapphire eyes, babbled of the stormy nights in the mountains around dad's cabin.

Old Jerome went immediately upstairs to hot-water-bottles and quinine. Nevada fluttered into the study, the only cheerfully lighted room, subsided into an armchair, and, while at the endless task of unbuttoning her elbow gloves, gave oral testimony as to the demerits of the "show."

"Yes, I think Mr. Fields[1] is really amusing—sometimes," said Barbara. "Here is a letter for you, dear, that came by special delivery just after you had gone."

"Who is it from?" asked Nevada, tugging at a button.

"Well, really," said Barbara, with a smile, "I can only guess. The envelope has that queer little thing in one corner that Gilbert calls a palette, but which looks to me rather like a gilt heart on a schoolgirl's valentine."

"I wonder what he's writing to me about," remarked Nevada, listlessly.

"We're all alike," said Barbara; "all women. We try to find out what is in a letter by studying the postmark. As a last resort we use scissors, and read it from the bottom upward. Here it is."

She made a motion as if to toss the letter across the table to Nevada.

"Great catamounts!" exclaimed Nevada. "These buttons are a nuisance. I'd rather wear buskskins. Oh, Barbara, please shuck the hide off that letter and read it. It'll be midnight before I get these gloves off!"

"Why, dear, you don't want me to open Gilbert's letter to you? It's for you, and you wouldn't wish any one else to read it, of course!"

Nevada raised her steady, calm, sapphire eyes from her gloves.

"Nobody writes me anything that everybody mightn't read," she said. "Go on, Barbara. Maybe Gilbert wants us to go out in his car again tomorrow."

Curiosity can do more things than kill a cat; and if emotions, well recognized as feminine, are harmful to feline life,

[1] Mr. Fields: W.C. Fields, for many years a comic actor.

then jealousy would soon leave the whole world catless. Barbara opened the letter, with a slightly bored air.

"Well, dear," she said, "I'll read it if you want me to."

She slit the envelope, and read the missive with swift-travelling eyes. She read it again, and cast a quick, shrewd glance at Nevada, who, for the time, seemed to consider gloves as the world of her interest, and letters from rising artists as no more than messages from Mars.

For a quarter of a minute Barbara looked at Nevada with a strange steadfastness. Then a smile so small that it widened her mouth only the sixteenth part of an inch, and narrowed her eyes no more than a twentieth flashed like an inspired thought across her face.

Since the beginning no woman has been a mystery to another woman. Swift as light travels, each penetrates the heart and mind of another, sifts her sister's words of their cunningest disguises, reads her most hidden desires.

Barbara seemed to hesitate.

"Really, Nevada," she said, with a little show of embarrassment, "you shouldn't have insisted on my opening this. I—I'm sure it wasn't meant for anyone else to know."

Nevada forgot her gloves for a moment.

"Then read it aloud," she said. "Since you've already read it, what's the difference? If Mr. Warren has written to me something that anyone else oughtn't to know, that is the more reason why everybody should know it."

"Well," said Barbara, "this is what is says: 'Dearest Nevada—Come to my studio at twelve o'clock tonight. Do not fail.'" Barbara rose and dropped the note in Nevada's lap. "I'm awfully sorry," she said, "that I knew. It isn't like Gilbert. There must be some mistake. Just consider that I am ignorant of it, will you, dear? I must go upstairs now, I have such a headache. I'm sure I don't understand the note. Perhaps Gilbert has been dining too well, and will explain. Good night!"

IV

Nevada tiptoed to the hall, and heard Barbara's door close upstairs. The bronze clock in the study told the hour of twelve was fifteen minutes away. She ran swiftly to the front door, and let herself out into the snowstorm. Gilbert Warren's studio was six blocks away.

Nevada plunged like a wind-driven storm-petrel on her way. She looked up at the cloud-capped buildings that rose above the streets, shaded by the night lights and the congealed vapors to gray, drab, ashen, lavender, and dun tints. They were so like the wintry mountains of her Western home that she felt a satisfaction such as the hundred-thousand-dollar house had seldom brought her.

A policeman caused her to waver on a corner, just by his eye and weight.

"Hello, Mabel!" said he. "Kind of late for you to be out, ain't it?"

"I—I am just going to the drugstore," said Nevada, hurrying past him.

The excuse serves as a passport for the most sophisticated.

Turning eastward, the direct blast cut down Nevada's speed one-half. She made zigzag tracks in the snow; but she was as tough as a sapling, and bowed to it as gracefully. Suddenly the studio-building loomed before her, a familiar landmark, like a cliff above some well-remembered canyon. The haunt of business and its hostile neighbor, art, was darkened and silent. The elevator stopped at ten.

Up eight flights of stairs Nevada climbed, and rapped firmly at the door numbered "89." She had been there many times before, with Barbara and Uncle Jerome.

Gilbert opened the door. He had a crayon pencil in one hand, a green shade over his eyes, and a pipe in his mouth. The pipe dropped to the floor.

"Am I late?" asked Nevada. "I came as quick as I could. Uncle and me were at the theater this evening. Here I am, Gilbert!"

Gilbert did a Pygmalion-and-Galatea[2] act. He changed from a statue of surprise to a young man with a problem to tackle. He admitted Nevada, got a whiskbroom, and began to brush the snow from her clothes. A great lamp, with a green shade, hung over an easel, where the artist had been sketching in crayon.

"You wanted me," said Nevada, simply, "and I came. You said so in your letter. What did you send for me for?"

"You read my letter?" inquired Gilbert, sparring for wind.

"Barbara read it to me. I saw it afterward. It said: 'Come to my studio at twelve tonight, and do not fail.' I thought you were sick, of course, but you don't seem to be."

"Aha!" said Gilbert. "I'll tell you why I asked you to come, Nevada. I want you to marry me immediately— tonight. What's a little snowstorm? Will you do it?"

"You might have noticed that I would, long ago," said Nevada. "And I'm rather stuck on the snowstorm idea,

---

[2] Pygmalion and Galatea: Pygmalion, a king and sculptor of Cyprus, who fell in love with an ivory statue of a girl he had made and named Galatea. A goddess brought the statue to life.

myself. I surely would hate one of those flowery church weddings. Gilbert, I didn't know you had grit enough to propose in this way. Let's shock 'em—it's our funeral, ain't it?"

"You bet!" said Gilbert. "Where did I hear that expression?" he added to himself. "Wait a minute, Nevada. I want to do a little phoning."

He shut himself up in a little dressing-room, and called.

"That you, Jack? You confounded sleepy-head! Yes, wake up. This is me—or I—oh, bother the difference in grammar! I'm going to be married right away. Yes! Wake up your sister—don't answer me back. Bring her along, too—you *must*. Remind Agnes of the time I saved her from drowning in Lake Ronkonkoma—I know it's nasty to refer to it, but she *must* come with you. Yes! Nevada is here, waiting. We've been engaged quite a while. Some opposition among the relatives, you know, and we have to pull it off this way. We're waiting here for you. Don't let Agnes out-talk you—bring her! You will? Good old boy! I'll order a carriage to call for you, double-quick time. Confound you, Jack, you're all right!"

Gilbert returned to the room where Nevada waited.

"My old friend, Jack Peyton, and his sister were to have been here at a quarter to twelve," he explained; "but Jack is so confoundedly slow. I've just phoned them to hurry. They'll be here in a few minutes. I'm the happiest man in the world, Nevada! What did you do with the letter I sent today?"

"I've got it cinched here," said Nevada, pulling it out from beneath her opera-cloak.

Gilbert drew the letter from the envelope and looked it over carefully. Then he looked at Nevada thoughtfully.

"Didn't you think it rather queer that I should ask you to come to my studio at midnight?" he asked.

"Why, no," said Nevada, rounding her eyes. "Not if you needed me. Out West, when a pal sends you a hurry call—ain't that what you say here?—we get there first and talk

113

about it after the row is over. And it's usually snowing there, too, when things happen. So I didn't mind."

Gilbert rushed into another room, and came back burdened with overcoats warranted to turn away wind, rain, or snow.

"Put this raincoat on," he said, holding it for her. "We have a quarter of a mile to go. Old Jack and his sister will be here in a few minutes." He began to struggle into a heavy coat. "Oh, Nevada," he said, "just look at the headlines on the front page of that evening paper on the table, will you? It's about your section of the West, and I know it will interest you."

He waited a full minute, pretending to find trouble in getting on of his overcoat, and then turned. Nevada had not moved. She was looking at him with strange and pensive directness. Her cheeks had a flush on them beyond the color that had been contributed by the wind and snow; but her eyes were steady.

"I was going to tell you," she said, "anyhow, before you—before we—before—well, before anything. Dad never gave me a day of schooling. I never learned to read or write a darned word. Now if—"

Pounding their uncertain way upstairs, the feet of Jack and Agnes were heard.

V

When Mr. and Mrs. Gilbert Warren were spinning softly homeward in a closed carriage, after the ceremony, Gilbert said:

"Nevada, would you really like to know what I wrote you in the letter that you received tonight?"

"Fire away!" said his bride.

"Word for word," said Gilbert, "it was this: 'My dear Miss Warren—You were right about the flower. It was a hydrangea, and not a lilac.'"

"All right," said Nevada. "But let's forget it. The joke's on Barbara, anyway!"

Rus in Urbe[1]

New York may not be the best summer resort in the world for everyone, but this time it seemed like a pretty good place to stay in, even in hot weather.

Considering men in relation to money, there are three kinds whom I dislike: men who have more money than they can spend; men who have more money than they do spend; and men who spend more money than they have. Of the three varieties, I believe I have the least liking for the first. But, as a man, I liked Spencer Grenville North pretty well although he had something like two or ten or thirty millions— I've forgotten exactly how many.

I did not leave town that summer. I usually went down to a village on the south shore of Long Island. The place was surrounded by duck-farms, and the ducks and dogs and whip-poor-wills and rusty wind-mills made so much noise that I could sleep as peacefully as if I were in my own flat six doors from the elevated railroad in New York. But that summer I did not go. Remember that. One of my friends asked me why I did not. I replied: "Because, old man, New York is the finest summer resort in the world." You have heard that phrase before. But that is what I told him.

I was press-agent that year for Binkley & Bing, the theatrical managers and producers. Of course you know what a press-agent is. Well, he is not. That is the secret of being one.

Binkley was touring France in his new car, and Bing had gone to Scotland to learn curling,[2] which he seemed to

[1] Rus in Urbe: the country in the city.
[2] Curling: a winter game played on the ice.

115

associate in his mind with hot tongs rather than with ice. Before they left they gave me June and July, on salary, for my vacation, which act was in accord with their large spirit of liberality. But I remained in New York, which I had decided was the finest summer resort in—

But I said that before.

On July the 10th, North came to town from his camp in the Adirondacks. Try to imagine a camp with sixteen rooms, plumbing, eiderdown quilts, a butler, a garage, solid silver plate, and a long-distance telephone. Of course it was in the woods.

North came to see me in my three rooms and bath, extra charge for light when used extravagantly or all night. He slapped me on the back (I would rather have my shins kicked any day), and greeted me with outdoor heartiness and revolting good spirits. He was insolently brown and healthy-looking, and offensively well dressed.

"Just ran down for a few days," said he, "to sign some papers and stuff like that. My lawyer wired me to come. Well, what are you doing in town? I took a chance and telephoned, and they said you were here. What's the matter with that Utopia on Long Island where you used to take your type-writer and your temper every summer? Anything wrong with the—er—swans, weren't they, that used to sing on the farms at night?"

"Ducks," said I. "The songs of swans are for luckier ears. They swim and curve their necks in artificial lakes on the estates of the wealthy to delight the eyes of the favorites of Fortune."

"Also in Central Park," said North, "to delight the eyes of immigrants and bummers. I've seen 'em there lots of times. But why are you in the city so late in the summer?"

"New York City," I began to recite, "is the finest sum—"

"No, you don't," said North, emphatically. "You don't spring that old one on me. I know you know better. Man, you ought to have gone up with us this summer. The Prestons

are there, and Tom Volney and the Monroes and Lulu Stan-
ford and the Miss Kennedy and her aunt that you liked so
well."

"I never liked Miss Kennedy's aunt," I said.

"I didn't say you did," said North. "We are having the
greatest time we've ever had. The pickerel and trout are so
hungry that I believe they would swallow your hook with a
Montana copper-mine prospectus fastened on it. And we've
a couple of electric launches; and I'll tell you what we do
every night or two—we tow a rowboat behind each one with
a big phonograph and a boy to change the discs in 'em.
On the water, and 20 yards behind you, they are not so bad.
And there are passably good roads through the woods where
we go motoring. I shipped two cars up there. And the Pinecliff Inn is only three miles away. You know the Pinecliff.
Some good people are there this season, and we run over to
the dances twice a week. Can't you go back with me for a
week, old man?"

I laughed. "Northy," said I—"if I may be so familiar with
a millionaire, because I hate both the names Spencer and
Grenville—your invitation is meant kindly, but—the city in
the summer-time is for me. Here, while the *bourgeoisie* is
away, I can live as Nero[3] lived—barring, thank Heaven, the
fiddling—while the city burns at ninety in the shade. The
tropics and the zones wait upon me like handmaidens. I sit
under Florida palms and eat pomegranates while Boreas[4]
himself, electrically powered, blows upon me his Arctic
breath. As for trout, you know yourself, that Jean, at
Maurice's, cooks them better than anyone else in the world."

"Be advised," said North. "My chef has pinched the blue
ribbon from the lot. He lays some slices of bacon inside the
trout, wraps it all in corn-husks—the husks of green corn,
you know—buries them in hot ashes and covers them with

[3] Nero: an emperor of Rome.
[4] Boreas: the ancient Greek personification of the north wind.

117

live coals. We build fires on the bank of the lake and have fish suppers."

"I know," said I. "And the servants bring down tables and chairs and damask cloths, and you eat with silver forks. I know the kind of camps that you millionaires have. And there are champagne pails set about, disgracing the wild flowers, and, no doubt, Madame Tetrazzini to sing in the boat pavilion after the trout."

"Oh, no," said North, concernedly, "we were never as bad as that. We did have a variety troupe up from the city three or four nights, but they weren't stars by as far as light can travel in the same length of time. I always like a few home comforts even when I'm roughing it. But don't tell me you prefer to stay in the city during summer. I don't believe it. If you do, why didn't you spend your summers there for the last four years, instead of sneaking away from town on a night train, and refusing to tell your friends where this Arcadian village was?"

"Because," said I, "they might have followed me and discovered it. But since then I have learned that Amaryllis[5] has come to town. The coolest things, the freshest, the brightest, the choicest, are to be found in the city. If you've nothing on hand this evening I will show you."

"I'm free," said North, "and I have my light car outside. I suppose, since you've been converted to the town, that your idea of rural sport is to have a little whirl between bicycle cops in Central Park and then a mug of sticky ale in some stuffy saloon under a fan that can't stir up as many revolutions in a week as Nicaragua can in a day."

"We'll begin with the spin through the Park, anyhow," I said. I was choking with the hot, stale air of my little apartment, and I wanted that breath of the cool to brace me for the task of proving to my friend that New York was the greatest—and so forth.

---

[5] Amaryllis: a traditional name for a Greek shepherdess.

"Where can you find air any fresher or purer than this?" I asked, as we sped into the park.

"Air!" said North, contemptuously. "Do you call this air?—this muggy vapor, smelling of garbage and gasoline smoke. Man, I wish you could get one sniff of the real Adirondack article in the pine woods at daylight."

"I have heard of it," said I. "But for fragrance and tang and a joy in the nostrils I would not give one puff of sea breeze across the bay, down on my little boat dock on Long Island, for ten of your turpentine-scented tornadoes."

"Then why," asked North, a little curiously, "don't you go there instead of staying cooped in this Greater Bakery?"

"Because," said I, doggedly, "I have discovered that New York is the greatest summer—"

"Don't say that again," interrupted North, "unless you've actually got a job as General Passenger Agent of the Subway. You can't really believe it."

I went to some trouble to try to prove my theory to my friend. The Weather Bureau and the season had conspired to make the argument worthy of an able supporter.

The city seemed stretched on a broiler directly above the furnaces of Avernus.[6] There was a kind of tepid gaiety afoot and awheel in the boulevards, mainly shown by men strolling about in straw hats and evening clothes, and rows of idle taxicabs with their flags up, looking like a blockaded Fourth of July procession. The hotels kept up a false brilliancy and hospitable outlook, but inside one saw vast empty caverns, and the footrails at the bars gleamed brightly from long absence of the sole-leather of customers. In the cross-town streets the steps of the old brown-stone houses were swarming with "stoopers," that motley race hailing from skylight room and basement, bringing out their straw door-step mats to sit and fill the air with strange noises and opinions.

North and I dined on the top of a hotel; and here, for

[6] Avernus: Hades or the infernal regions.

a few minutes, I thought I had made a point. An east wind, almost cool, blew across the roofless roof. A capable orchestra concealed in a bower of wisteria played with sufficient judgment to make the art of music probable and the art of conversation possible.

Some ladies in reproachless summer gowns at other tables gave life and color to the scene. And an excellent dinner, mainly from the refrigerator, seemed to successfully back my judgment as to summer resorts. But North grumbled all during the meal, and cursed his lawyers and prated so of his confounded camp in the woods that I began to wish he would go back there and leave me in my peaceful city retreat.

After dining we went to a roof-garden show that was being much praised. There we found a good bill, an artificially cooled atmosphere, cold drinks, prompt service, and a gay, well-dressed audience. North was bored.

"If this isn't comfortable enough for you on the hottest August night for five years," I said, a little sarcastically, "you

might think about the kids down in Delancey and Hester streets lying out on the fire-escapes with their tongues hanging out, trying to get a breath of air that hasn't been fried on both sides. The contrast might increase your enjoyment."

"Don't talk Socialism," said North. "I gave five hundred dollars to the free ice fund on the first day of May. I'm contrasting these stale, artifical, hollow, wearisome 'amusements' with the enjoyment a man can get in the woods. You should see the firs and pines do skirt-dances during a storm; and lie down flat and drink out of a mountain branch at the end of a day's tramp after the deer. That's the only way to spend a summer. Get out and live with Nature."

"I agree with you absolutely," said I, with emphasis.

For one moment I had relaxed my vigilance, and had spoken my true sentiments. North looked at me long and curiously.

"Then why, in the name of Pan and Apollo," he asked, "have you been singing this deceitful paean to summer in town?"

I suppose I looked my guilt.

"Ha," said North, "I see. May I ask her name?"

"Annie Ashton," said I, simply. "She played Nanette in Binkley & Bing's production of 'The Silver Cord.' She is to have a better part next season."

"Take me to see her," said North.

Miss Ashton lived with her mother in a small hotel. They were out of the West, and had a little money that bridged the seasons. As press-agent of Binkley & Bing I had tried to keep her before the public. As Robert James Vandiver, I had hoped to withdraw her. If ever one was made to keep company with said Vandiver and smell the salt breeze on the south shore of Long Island and listen to the ducks quack in the watches of the night, it was the Ashton set forth above.

But she had a soul above ducks—above nightingales. Aye, even above the birds of paradise. She was very beautiful, with quiet ways, and seemed genuine. She had both taste and talent for the stage, and she liked to stay at home and read and make caps for her mother. She was always kind and friendly with Binkley & Bing's press-agent. Since the theater had closed she had allowed Mr. Vandiver to call in an unofficial role. I had often spoken to her of my friend, Spencer Grenville North. And so, as it was early, the first turn of the vaudeville being not yet over, we left to find a telephone.

Miss Ashton would be very glad to see Mr. Vandiver and Mr. North.

We found her fitting a new cap on her mother. I never saw her look more charming.

North made himself disagreeably entertaining. He was a good talker and had a way with him. Besides, he had two, ten, or thirty millions. I've forgotten which. I carelessly admired the mother's cap, whereupon she brought out her store of a dozen or two, and I took a course in edgings and frills. Even though Annie's fingers had pinked, or ruched, or hemmed, or whatever you do to 'em, they palled upon me. And I could hear North drivelling to Annie about his Adirondack camp.

Two days after that I saw North in his motor-car with Miss Ashton and her mother. On the next afternoon he dropped in on me.

"Bobby," said he, "this old burg isn't such a bad proposition in the summertime, after all. Since I've been knocking around it looks better to me. There are some first-rate musical comedies and light operas on the roofs and in the outdoor gardens. And if you hunt up the first places and stick to soft drinks, you can keep about as cool here as you can in the country. Hang it! when you come to think of it, there's nothing much to the country, anyhow. You get tired and sunburned and lonesome, and you have to eat any old thing that the cook dishes up to you."

"It makes a difference, doesn't it?" said I.

"It certainly does. Now, I found some whitebait yesterday, at Maurice's, with a new sauce that beats anything in the trout line I ever tasted."

"It makes a difference, doesn't it?" I asked, looking him straight in the eye. He understood.

"Look here, Bob," he said, "I was going to tell you. I couldn't help it. I'll play fair with you, but I'm going to win. She is the 'one particular' for me."

"All right," said I. "It's a fair field. There are no rights for you to encroach upon."

On Thursday afternoon Miss Ashton invited North and myself to have tea in her apartment. He was devoted, and she was more charming than usual. By avoiding the subject of caps I managed to get a word or two into and out of the talk. Miss Ashton asked me in a make-conversational tone something about the next season's tour.

"Oh," said I, "I don't know about that. I'm not going to be with Binkley & Bing next season."

"Why, I thought," said she, "that they were going to put Number One road company under your charge. I thought you told me so."

"They were," said I, "but they won't. I'll tell you what I'm going to do. I'm going to the south shore of Long Island and buy a small cottage on the edge of the bay. And I'll buy a catboat and a rowboat and a shotgun and a yellow dog. I've got money enough to do it. And I'll smell the salt wind all day when it blows from the sea and the pine odor when it blows from the land. And, of course, I'll write plays until I have a trunk full of 'em on hand.

"And the next thing and the biggest thing I'll do will be to buy that duck-farm next door. Few people understand ducks. I can watch 'em for hours. They can march better than any company in the National Guard. They can play 'follow my leader' better than the entire Democratic party. Their voices don't amount to much, but I like to hear 'em. They wake you up a dozen times a night, but there's a homely sound about their quacking that is more musical to me than the cry of 'Fresh strawber-rees!' under your window in the morning when you want to sleep.

"And," I went on, enthusiastically, "do you know the

value of ducks besides their beauty and intelligence and order and sweetness of voice? Picking their feathers gives an unfailing and never-ceasing income. On a farm that I know the feathers were sold for $400 in one year. Think of that! And the ones shipped to the market will bring in more money than that. Yes, I think I shall get a cook, and with him and the dog and the sunsets for company I shall do well. No more of this dull, baking, senseless, roaring city for me."

Miss Ashton looked surprised. North laughed.

"I am going to begin one of my plays tonight," I said, "so I must be going." And with that I took my leave.

A few days later Miss Ashton telephoned, asking me to call at four in the afternoon. I did.

"You have been very good to me," she said, hesitatingly, "and I thought I would tell you. I am going to leave the stage."

"Yes," said I, "I suppose you will. They usually do when there's so much money."

"There is no money," she said, "or very little. Our money is almost gone."

"But I am told," said I, "that he has something like two or ten or thirty millions—I have forgotten which."

"I know what you mean," she said. "I will not pretend that I do not. I am not going to marry Mr. North."

"Then why are you leaving the stage?" I asked, severely. "What else can you do to earn a living?"

She came closer to me, and I can see the look in her eyes as she spoke.

"I can pick ducks," she said.

We sold the first year's feathers for $350.

"Girl"

It took a detective to locate the girl and both persuasion and a bribe from Hartley to win her consent—to what?

In gilt letters on the ground glass of the door of room 962 were the words: "Robbins & Hartley, Brokers." The clerks had gone. It was past five, and with the solid tramp of a drove of prize Percherons,[1] scrub-women were invading the cloud-capped 20 story office building. A puff of red-hot air flavored with lemon peelings, soft-coal smoke, and train oil came in through the half-open windows.

Robbins, 50, something of an overweight beau, and addicted to first nights and hotel palm-rooms, pretended to be envious of his partner's commuter's joys.

"Going to be something doing in the humidity line to-night," he said. "You out-of-town chaps will be the people, with your katydids and moonlight and long drinks and things out on the front porch."

Hartley, 29, serious, thin, good-looking, nervous, sighed and frowned a little.

"Yes," said he, "we always have cool nights in Floralhurst, especially in the winter."

A man with an air of mystery came in the door and went up to Hartley.

"I've found where she lives," he announced in the half-whisper that makes the detective at work a marked being to his fellow men.

Hartley scowled him into a state of dramatic silence and

---

[1] Percherons: a breed of horses.

quietude. But by that time Robbins had got his tie pin to his liking, and with a nod went out to his metropolitan amusements.

"Here is the address," said the detective in a natural tone, lacking an audience to foil.

Hartley took the leaf torn out of the sleuth's dingy notebook. On it were penciled the words "Vivienne Arlington, No. 341 East—th Street, care of Mrs. McComus."

"Moved there a week ago," said the detective. "Now if you want any shadowing done, Mr. Hartley, I can do you as fine a job in that line as anybody in the city. It will be only $7 a day and expenses. Can send in a daily type-written report, covering—"

"You needn't go on," interrupted the broker. "It isn't a case of that kind. I merely wanted the address. How much shall I pay you?"

"One day's work," said the sleuth. "A tenner will cover it."

Hartley paid the man and dismissed him. Then he left the office and boarded a Broadway car. At the first large crosstown street he took an east-bound car that deposited him in a decaying avenue, whose ancient structures once sheltered the pride and glory of the town.

Walking a few squares, he came to the building that he sought. It was a new flat-house, bearing its name carved upon its cheap stone portal. Fire-escapes zigzagged down its front— these laden with household goods, drying clothes, and squalling children evicted by the midsummer heat. Here and there a pale rubber plant peeped from the mass as if wondering to what kingdom it belonged—vegetable, animal, or artificial.

Hartley pressed the "McComus" button. The door latch clicked—now hospitably, now doubtfully, as though in anxiety whether it might be admitting friends or foes. Hartley entered and began to climb the stairs after the manner of a boy who climbs an apple-tree, stopping when he comes upon what he wants.

On the fourth floor he saw Vivienne standing in an open door. She invited him inside, with a nod and a bright, genuine smile. She placed a chair for him near a window, and poised herself gracefully upon the edge of one of those pieces of furniture that are masked and mysteriously hooded, unguessable bulks by day and racks of torture by night.

Hartley cast a quick, critical, appreciative glance at her before speaking, and told himself that his taste in choosing had been perfect.

Vivienne was about 21. She was of the purest Saxon type. Her hair was a ruddy golden. In perfect harmony were her ivory-clear complexion and deep sea-blue eyes that looked upon the world with the calmness of a mermaid or the pixie of an undiscovered mountain stream. Her frame was strong and yet possessed the grace of absolute naturalness. And yet with all her Northern clearness and frankness of line and coloring, there seemed to be something of the tropics in her—something of languor in the droop of her pose, of love of ease, of satisfaction and comfort in the mere act of breathing—something that seemed to claim for her a right as a perfect work of nature to exist and be admired equally with a rare flower or some beautiful, milk-white dove among its sober-hued companions.

She was dressed in a white blouse and dark skirt—that discreet masquerade of goose-girl and duchess.

"Vivienne," said Hartley, looking at her pleadingly, "you did not answer my last letter. It was only by nearly a week's search that I found where you had moved to. Why have you kept me in suspense when you knew how anxiously I was waiting to see you and hear from you?"

The girl looked out the window dreamily.

"Mr. Hartley," she said hesitatingly, "I hardly know what to say to you. I realize all the advantages of your offer, and sometimes I feel sure that I could be contented with you. But, again, I am doubtful. I was born a city girl, and I am afraid to bind myself to a quiet suburban life."

"My dear girl," said Hartley, ardently, "have I not told you that you shall have everything that your heart can desire that is in my power to give you? You shall come to the city for the theaters, for shopping, and to visit your friends as often as you care to. You can trust me, can you not?"

"To the fullest," she said, turning her frank eyes upon him with a smile. "I know you are the kindest of men, and that the girl you get will be a lucky one. I learned all about you when I was at the Montgomerys'."

"Ah!" exclaimed Hartley, with a tender light in his eye; "I remember well the evening I first saw you at the Montgomerys'. Mrs. Montgomery was sounding your praises to me all the evening. And she hardly did you justice. I shall never forget that supper. Come, Vivienne, promise me. I want you. You'll never regret coming with me. No one else will ever give you as pleasant a home."

The girl sighed and looked down at her folded hands.

A sudden jealous suspicion seized Hartley.

"Tell me, Vivienne," he asked, regarding her keenly, "is there another—is there someone else?"

A rosy flush crept slowly over her fair cheeks and neck.

"You shouldn't ask that, Mr. Hartley," she said, in some confusion. "But I will tell you. There is one other—but he has no right—I have promised him nothing."

"His name?" demanded Hartley, sternly.

"Townsend."

"Rafford Townsend!" exclaimed Hartley, with a grim tightening of his jaw. "How did that man come to know you? After all I've done for him—"

"His auto has just stopped below," said Vivienne, bending over the window-sill. "He's coming for his answer. Oh, I don't know what to do!"

The bell in the flat kitchen whirred. Vivienne hurried to press the latch button.

"Stay here," said Hartley. "I will meet him in the hall."

Townsend, looking like a Spanish grandee in his light

tweeds, Panama hat, and curling black mustache, came up the stairs three at a time. He stopped at sight of Hartley and looked foolish.

"Go back," repeated Hartley, harshly. "The Law of the Jungle. Do you want the Pack to tear you to pieces? The kill is mine."

"I came here to see a plumber about the bathroom pipes," said Townsend, bravely.

"All right," said Hartley. "You shall have that lying plaster to stick upon your soul. But, go back."

Townsend went downstairs, leaving a bitter word to be wafted up the stair-case. Hartley went back to his wooing.

"Vivienne," said he, masterfully, "I have got to have you. I will take no more refusals or dilly-dallying."

"When do you want me?" she asked.

"Now. As soon as you can get ready."

She stood calmly before him and looked him in the eye.

"Do you think for one moment," she said, "that I would enter your home while Héloise is there?"

Hartley cringed as if from an unexpected blow. He folded his arms and paced the carpet once or twice.

"She shall go," he declared, grimly. Drops stood upon his brow. "Why should I let that woman make my life miserable? Never have I seen one day of freedom from trouble since I have known her. You are right, Vivienne. Héloise must be sent away before I can take you home. But she shall go. I have decided. I will turn her from my doors."

"When will you do this?" asked the girl.

Hartley clinched his teeth and bent his brows together.

"Tonight," he said, resolutely. "I will send her away tonight."

"Then," said Vivienne, "my answer is 'yes.' Come for me when you will."

She looked into his eyes with a sweet, sincere light in her own. Hartley could scarcely believe that her surrender was true, it was so swift and complete.

"Promise me," he said, feelingly, "on your word and honor."

"On my word and honor," repeated Vivienne, softly.

At the door he turned and gazed at her happily, but yet as one who scarcely trusts the foundations of his joy.

"Tomorrow," he said.

"Tomorrow," she repeated with a smile of truth and candor.

In an hour and forty minutes Hartley stepped off the train at Floralhurst. A brisk walk of ten minutes brought him to the gate of a handsome two-story cottage set upon a wide and well-tended lawn. Halfway to the house he was met by a woman with jet-black braided hair and flowing white summer gown, who half strangled him without apparent cause.

When they stepped into the hall she said:

"Mamma's here. The auto is coming for her in half an hour. She came to dinner, but there's no dinner."

"I've something to tell you," said Hartley. "I thought to break it to you gently, but since your mother is here we may as well out with it."

He stooped and whispered something at her ear.

His wife screamed. Her mother came running into the hall. The dark-haired woman screamed again—the joyful scream of a well-beloved and petted woman.

"Oh, mamma!" she cried, ecstatically, "what do you think? Vivienne is coming to cook for us! She is the one that stayed with the Montgomerys a whole year. And now, Billy, dear," she concluded, "you must go right down into the kitchen and fire Héloise. She has been drunk again the whole day long."

The Whirligig
of Life

The amazing adventure of a five-dollar bill, and the way it helped to make two people unhappy and then to bring happiness back to them.

Justice of the Peace Benaja Widdup sat in the door of his office smoking his elder-stem pipe. The Cumberland range rose blue-gray in the afternoon haze. A speckled hen swaggered down the main street of the "settlement," crackling foolishly.

Up the road came a sound of creaking axles, and then a slow cloud of dust, and then a bull-cart bearing Ransie Bilbro and his wife. The cart sopped at the Justice's door, and the two climbed down. Ransie was a narrow six feet of sallow brown skin and yellow hair. The calmness of the mountains hung upon him like a suit of armor. The woman was calicoed, angled, snuff-brushed, and weary with unknown desires. Through it all gleamed a faint protest of cheated youth unconscious of its loss.

The Justice of the Peace slipped his feet into his shoes, for the sake of dignity, and moved to let them enter.

"We-all," said the woman in a voice like the wind blowing through pine boughs, "wants a divo'ce." She looked at Ransie to see if he noted any flaw or evasion or partiality or self-partnership in her statement of their business.

"A divo'ce," repeated Ransie, with a solemn nod. "We-all can't git along together nohow. It's lonesome enough fur to live in the mountins when a man and a woman keers fur one another. But when she's a-spittin' like a wildcat or a-sullenin' like a hoot-owl in the cabin, a man an't got no call to live with her."

"When he's a no-'count varmint," said the woman, without any especial warmth, "a traipsin' along of scalawags and moonshiners and a-layin' on his back pizen 'ith co'n whiskey, and a-pesterin' folks with a pack o'hungry, triflin houn's to feed!"

"When she keeps a-throwin' skillet lids," came Ransie's reply, "and slings b'ilin water on the best coon-dog in the Cumberlands, and sets herself again' cookin' a man's victuals, and keeps him awake o' nights accusin' him of a sight of doin's!"

"When he's al'ays a-fightin' the revenues, and gits a hard name in the mount'ins fur a mean man, who's gwine to be able fur to sleep o' nights?"

The Justice of the Peace stirred deliberately to his duties. He placed his one chair and a wooden stool for his petitioners. He opened his book of statutes on the table and scanned the index. Presently he wiped his spectacles and shifted his inkstand.

"The law and the statutes," said he, "air silent on the subjeck of divo'ce as fur as the jurisdiction of this co't air concerned. But, accordin' to equity and the ways, if a justice of the peace can marry a couple, it's plain that he is bound to be able to divo'ce 'em. This here office will issue a decree of divo'ce."

Ransie Bilbro drew a small tabacco-bag from his pocket. Out of this he shook upon the table a five-dollar note. "Sold a b'arskin and two foxes fur that," he remarked. "It's all the money we got."

"The regular price of a divo'ce in this co't," said the Justice, "air five dollars." He stuffed the bill into the pocket of his homespun vest with an air of indifference. With much bodily toil and mental hardship he wrote the decree upon half a sheet of foolscap, and then copied it upon the other. Ransie Bilbro and his wife listened to his reading of the document that was to give them freedom:

"Know all men by these presents that Ransie Bilbro and his wife, Ariela Bilbro, this day personally appeared before me and promises that hereinafter they will neither love, honor, nor obey each other, neither for better nor worse, being of sound mind and body, and accept summons for divorce according to the peace and dignity of the State. Herein fail not, so help you God. Benaja Widdup, justice of the peace in and for the county of Piedmont, State of Tennessee."

The Justice was about to hand one of the documents to Ransie. The voice of Ariela delayed the transfer. Both men looked at her. Their dull masculinity was confronted by something sudden and unexpected in the woman.

"Judge, don't you give him that air paper yit. 'Taint all settled, nohow. I got to have my rights first. I got to have my ali-money. 'Taint no kind of a way to do fur a man to divo'ce his wife 'thout her havin' a cent fur to do with. I'm a-layin' off to be a-goin' up to brother Ed's up on Hogback Mount'in. I'm bound fur to hev a pa'r of shoes and some snuff and things besides. Ef Rance kin affo'd a divo'ce, let him pay me ali-money."

Ransie Bilbro was stricken dumb. There had been no previous hint of alimony. Women were always bringing up startling and unlooked-for issues.

Justice Benaja Widdup felt that the point demanded a decision. The authorities were also silent on the subject of alimony. But the woman's feet were bare. The trail to Hogback Mountain was steep and rough.

"Ariela Bilbro," he asked, in official tones, "how much did you 'low would be good and sufficient ali-money in the case befo' the co't?"

"I 'lowed," she answered, "fur the shoes and all, to say five dollars. That ain't much fur ali-money, but I reckon that'll git me up to brother Ed's."

"The amount," said the Justice, "air not onreasonable. Ransie Bilbro, you air ordered by the co't to pay the plaintiff the sum of five dollars befo' the decree of divo'ce air issued."

"I hain't no mo' money," breathed Ransie, heavily. "I done paid you all I had."

"Otherwise," said the Justice, looking severely over his spectacles, "you air in contempt of co't."

"I reckon if you gimme till tomorrow," pleaded the husband, "I mout be able to rake or scrape it up somewhars. I never looked for to be a-payin' no ali-money."

"The case air adjourned," said Benaja Widdup, "till tomorrow, when you-all will present yo'selves and obey the order of the co't. Followin' of which the decrees of divo'ce will be delivered." He sat down in the door and began to loosen a shoestring.

"We mout as well go down to Uncle Ziah's," decided Ransie, "and spend the night." He climbed into the cart on one side, and Ariela climbed in on the other. Obeying the flap of his rope, the little red bull slowly came around on a tack, and the cart crawled away.

Justice of the Peace Benaja Widdup smoked his elder-stem pipe. Late in the afternoon he got his weekly paper, and read it until the twilight dimmed its lines. Then he lit the candle on his table, and read until the moon rose, marking the time for supper. He lived in the double log cabin on the slope near the girdled poplar. Going home to supper he crossed a little branch darkened by a laural thicket. The dark figure of a man stepped from the laurels and pointed a rifle at his breast. His hat was pulled down low, and something covered most of his face.

"I want yo' money," said the figure. "'thout any talk. I'm gettin' nervous, and my finger's a-wabblin' on this here trigger."

"I've only got f-f-five dollars," said the Justice, producing it from his vest pocket.

"Roll it up," came the order, "and stick it in the end of this here gun-bar'l."

The bill was crisp and new. Even fingers that were clumsy and trembling found little difficulty in making a spill of it and inserting it (this with less ease) into the muzzle of the rifle.

"Now I reckon you kin be goin' along," said the robber.

The Justice lingered not on his way.

The next day came the little red bull, drawing the cart to the office door. Justice Benaja Widdup had his shoes on, for he was expecting the visit. In his presence Ransie Bilbro handed to his wife a five-dollar bill. The official's eye sharply viewed it. It seemed to curl up as though it had been rolled and inserted into the end of a gun-barrel. But the Justice refrained from comment. It is true that other bills might be inclined to curl. He handed each one a decree of divorce. Each stood awkwardly silent, slowly folding the guarantee of freedom. The woman cast a shy glance full of constraint at Ransie.

"I reckon you'll be goin' up to the cabin," she said, "along 'ith the bull-cart. There's bread in the tin box settin' on the shelf. I put the bacon in the b'ilin'-pot to keep the hounds from gettin' it. Don't forget to wind the clock tonight."

"You air a-goin' to your brother Ed's?" asked Ransie, with fine unconcern.

"I was 'lowin' to get along up thar afore night. I ain't sayin' as they'll pester theyselves any to make me welcome, but I han't nowhar else fur to go. It's a right smart ways, and I reckon I better be goin'. I'll be a sayin' good-bye, Ranse—that is, if you keer fur to say so."

"I don't know as anybody's a hound dog," said Ransie, in a martyr's voice, "fur to not want to say good-bye—'less you air so anxious to git away that you don't want me to say it."

Ariela was silent. She folded the five-dollar bill and her decree carefully, and placed them in the bosom of her dress. Benaja Widdup watched the money disappear with mournful eyes behind his spectacles.

And then with his next words he achieved rank (as his thoughts ran) with either the great crowd of the world's sympathizers or the little crowd of its great financiers.

"Be kind o'lonesome in the cabin tonight, Ransie," he said.

Ransie Bilbro stared out at the Cumberlands, clear blue now in the sunlight. He did not look at Ariela.

"I 'low it might be lonesome," he said; "but when folks gits mad and wants a divo'ce, you can't make folks stay."

"There's others wanted a divo'ce," said Ariela, speaking to the wooden stool. "Besides, nobody don't want nobody to stay."

"Nobody never said they didn't."

"Nobody never said they did. I reckon I better start on now to brother Ed's."

"Nobody can't wind that old clock."

"Want me to go along 'ith you in the cart and wind it fur you, Ranse?"

The mountaineer's face was proof against emotion. But he reached out a big hand and enclosed Ariela's thin brown one. Her soul peeped out once through her impassive face, hallowing it.

"Them hounds sha'n't pester you no more," said Ransie. "I reckon I been mean and low down. You wind that clock, Ariela."

"My heart hit's in that cabin, Ranse," she whispered, "along 'ith you. I ain't a-goin' to git mad no more. Le's be startin', Ranse, so's we kin git home by sundown."

Justice of the Peace Benaja Widdup blocked them as they started for the door, forgetting his presence.

"In the name of the State of Tennessee," he said, "I forbid you all to be a-defyin' of its laws and statutes. This co't is mo' than willin' and full of joy to see the clouds of discord and misunderstandin' rollin' away from two lovin' hearts. But it air the duy of the co't to p'eserve the morals and integrity of the State. The co't reminds you that you

138

air no longer man and wife, but air divorced by regular decree, and as such air not entitled to the benefits of the mattermonial estate."

Ariela caught Ransie's arm. Did those words mean that she must lose him now when they had just learned the lesson of life?

"But the co't air prepared," went on the Justice, "fur to remove the disabilities set up by the decree of divo'ce. The co't air on hand to perform the solemn ceremony of marri'ge, thus fixin' things up and enablin' the parties in the case to resume the honor'ble and elevatin' state of mattermony which they desires. The fee fur performin' said ceremony will be, in this case, to wit, five dollars."

Ariela caught the gleam of promise in his words. Swiftly her hand went to her bosom. Freely as an alighting dove the bill fluttered to the Justice's table. Her sallow cheek colored as she stood hand in hand with Ransie and listened to the reuniting words.

Ransie helped her into the cart, and climbed in beside her. The little red bull turned once more, and they set out, hand-clasped, for the mountains.

Justice of the Peace Benaja Widdup sat in his door and took off his shoes. Once again he fingered the bill tucked down in his vest pocket. Once again he smoked his elder-stem pipe. Once again the speckled hen swaggered down the main street cackling foolishly.

A Lickpenny Lover

It was love at first sight for the millionaire, but he didn't really understand his Masie.

There were 3,000 girls in the Biggest Store. Masie was one of them. She was eighteen and a saleslady in the gents' gloves. Here she became versed in two varieties of human beings—the kind of gents who buy their gloves in department stores and the kind of women who buy gloves for unfortunate gents. Besides this wide knowledge of the human species, Masie had acquired other information. She had listened to the wisdom of the 2,999 other girls and had stored it in a brain that was as secretive and wary as that of a Maltese cat. Perhaps nature, foreseeing that she would lack wise counsellors, had mingled the saving ingredient of shrewdness along with her beauty, as she has endowed the silver fox of the priceless fur above the other animals with cunning.

For Masie was beautiful. She was a deep-tinted blonde, with the calm poise of a lady who cooks butter cakes in a window. She stood behind her counter in the Biggest Store; and as you closed your hand over the tape-line for your glove measure you thought of Hebe[1]; and as you looked again you wondered how she had come by Minerva's[2] eyes.

When the floorwalker was not looking, Masie chewed candies. When he was looking she gazed up as if at the clouds and smiled wistfully.

[1] Hebe: a Greek goddess noted for her beauty.
[2] Minerva: Greek goddess of wisdom.

That is the shopgirl smile, and I urge you to shun it unless you are well fortified with a hard heart, caramels, and a congeniality for the capers of Cupid. This smile belonged to Masie's recreation hours and not to the store. But the floor-walker must have his own. He is the Shylock[3] of the stores. When he comes nosing around, the bridge of his nose is a toll-bridge. It is goo-goo eyes or "git" when he looks toward a pretty girl. Of course not all floorwalkers are thus. Only a few days ago the papers printed news of one over 80 years of age.

One day Irving Carter, painter, millionaire, traveler, poet, automobilist, happened to enter the Biggest Store. It is due to him to add that his visit was not voluntary. Filial duty took him by the collar and dragged him inside, while his mother wandered among the bronze and terra-cotta statuettes.

Carter strolled across to the glove counter in order to shoot a few minutes on the wing. His need for gloves was genuine; he had forgotten to bring a pair with him. But his action hardly calls for apology, because he had never heard of glove-counter flirtations.

As he neared the vicinity of his fate he hesitated, suddenly conscious of this unknown phase of Cupid's less worthy profession.

Three or four cheap fellows, loudly garbed, were leaning over the counters, wrestling with the hand-coverings, while giggling girls played vivacious seconds to their lead upon the strident string of coquetry. Carter would have retreated, but he had gone too far. Masie confronted him behind her counter with a questioning look in eyes as coldly, beautifully, warmly blue as the glint of summer sunshine on an iceberg drifting in Southern seas.

And then Irving Carter, painter, millionaire, etc., felt a warm flush rise to his aristocratically pale face. But not from shyness. The blush was intellectual in origin. He knew in a

[3] Shylock: one of the characters in Shakespeare's play, *The Merchant of Venice*.

moment that he stood in the ranks of the ready-made youths who wooed the giggling girls at other counters. Himself leaned against the oaken trysting place of a cockney Cupid with a desire in his heart for the favor of a glove salesgirl. He was no more than Bill and Jack and Mickey. And then he felt a sudden tolerance for them, and an elating, courageous contempt for the conventions upon which he had fed, and an unhesitating determination to have this perfect creature for his own.

When the gloves were paid for and wrapped Carter lingered for a moment. The dimples at the corners of Masie's mouth deepened. All gentlemen who bought gloves lingered in just that way. She curved an arm, and rested an elbow upon the showcase edge.

Carter had never before been in a situation of which he had not been perfect master. But now he stood far more awkward than Bill or Jack or Mickey. He had no chance of meeting this beautiful girl socially. His mind struggled to recall the nature and habits of shopgirls as he had read or heard of them. Somehow he had received the idea that they sometimes did not insist too strictly upon the regular channels of introduction. His heart beat loudly at the thought of proposing a meeting with this lovely being. But the tumult in his heart gave him courage.

After a few friendly and well-received remarks on general subjects, he laid his card by her hand on the counter.

"Will you please pardon me," he said, "if I seem too bold. But I earnestly hope you will allow me the pleasure of seeing you again. There is my name. I assure you that it is with the greatest respect that I ask the favor of becoming one of your fr—acquaintances. May I not hope for the privilege?"

Masie knew men—especially men who buy gloves. Without hesitation she looked him frankly and smilingly in the eyes and said:

"Sure. I guess you're all right. I don't usually go out with strange gentlemen, though. It ain't ladylike. When should you want to see me again?"

"As soon as I may," said Carter. "If you would allow me to call at your home, I—"

Masie laughed musically. "Oh, gee no!" she said, emphatically. "If you could see our flat once! There's five of us in three rooms. I'd just like to see ma's face if I was to bring a gentleman friend there!"

"Anywhere, then," said the enamored Carter, "that will be convenient to you."

"Say," suggested Masie, with a bright-idea look in her peach-blow face; "I guess Thursday night will about suit me. Suppose you come to the corner of Eighth Avenue and Forty-eighth Street at 7:30. I live right near the corner. But I've got to be back home by eleven. Ma never lets me stay out after eleven."

Carter promised gratefully to keep the date, and then hastened to his mother, who was looking about for him to ratify her purchase of a bronze Diana.

A salesgirl, with small eyes and an obtuse nose, strolled near Masie, with a friendly leer.

"Did you make a hit with his nobs, Masie?" she asked, familiarly.

"The gentleman asked permission to call," answered Masie, with the grand air, as she slipped Carter's card into the bosom of her dress.

"Permission to call!" echoed small eyes, with a snigger. "Did he say anything about dinner in the Waldorf and a spin in his auto afterward?"

"Oh, cheese it!" said Masie, wearily. "You've been used to swell things, I don't think. You've had a swelled head ever since that hosecart driver took you out to a chop suey joint. No, he never mentioned the Waldorf; but there's a Fifth Avenue address on his card."

As Carter glided away from the Biggest Store with his mother in his electric runabout, he bit his lip with a dull pain at his heart. He knew that love had come to him for the first time in all the 29 years of his life. And that the object of it should make so readily an appointment with him at a street corner, though it was a step toward his desires, tortured him with misgivings.

Carter did not know the shopgirl. He did not know that her home is often either a scarcely habitable tiny room or filled to overflowing with kith and kin. The street corner is her parlor. The park is her drawing room. The avenue is her garden walk.

One evening at dusk, two weeks after their first meeting, Carter and Masie strolled arm-in-arm into a little, dimly lit park. They found a bench, tree shadowed and secluded and sat there.

For the first time his arm stole gently around her. Her golden-bronze head slid restfully against his shoulder.

"Gee!" sighed Masie, thankfully. "Why didn't you ever think of that before?"

"Masie," said Carter, earnestly, "you surely know that I love you. I ask you sincerely to marry me. You know me well enough by this time to have no doubts of me. I want you, and I must have you. I care nothing for the difference in our stations."

"What is the difference?" asked Masie, curiously.

"Well, there isn't any," said Carter, quickly, "except in the minds of foolish people. It is in my power to give you a life of luxury. My social position is beyond dispute, and my means are ample."

"They all say that," remarked Masie. "It's the kid they all give you. I suppose you really work in a delicatessen or follow the races. I ain't as green as I look."

"I can furnish you all the proofs you want," said Carter, gently. "And I want you, Masie. I loved you the first day I saw you."

"They all do," said Masie, with an amused laugh, "to hear 'em talk. If I could meet a man that got stuck on me the third time he'd seen me I think I'd get mashed on him."

"Please don't say such things," pleaded Carter. "Listen to me, dear. Ever since I first looked into your eyes you have been the only woman in the world for me."

"Oh, ain't you the kidder!" smiled Masie. "How many other girls did you ever tell that?"

But Carter persisted. And at length he reached the flimsy fluttering little soul of the shopgirl that existed somewhere deep down in her lovely bosom. His words penetrated the heart whose very lightness was its safest armor. She looked up at him with eyes that saw. And a warm glow visited her cool cheeks. Tremblingly, awfully, her moth wings closed, and she seemed about to settle upon the flower of love. Some faint glimmer of life and its possibilities on the other side of her glove counter dawned upon her. Carter felt the change and crowded the opportunity.

"Marry me, Masie," he whispered, softly, "and we will go away from this ugly city to beautiful ones. We will forget work and business, and life will be one long holiday. I know where I should take you—I have been there often. Just think of a shore where summer is eternal, where the waves are always rippling on the lovely beach and the people are happy and free as children. We will sail to those shores and remain there as long as you please. In one of those far-away cities there are grand and lovely palaces and towers full of beautiful pictures and statues. The streets of the city are water, and one travels about in—"

"I know," said Masie, sitting up suddenly. "Gondolas."

"Yes," smiled Carter.

"I thought so," said Masie.

"And then," continued Carter, "we will travel on and see whatever we wish in the world. After the European cities we will visit India and the ancient cities there. We will ride on elephants and see the wonderful temples of the Hindoos and the Brahmins and the Japanese gardens and the camel trains and chariot races in Persia, and all the queer sights of foreign countries. Don't you think you would like it, Masie?"

Masie rose to her feet.

"I think we had better be going home," she said, cooly. "It's getting late."

Carter humored her. He had come to know her varying moods, and that it was useless to combat them. But he felt a certain happy triumph. He had held for a moment, though but by a silken thread, the soul of his wild Psyche, and hope was stronger within him. Once she had folded her wings and her cool hand had closed about his own.

At the Biggest Store the next day Masie's chum, Lulu, waylaid her in an angle of the counter.

"How are you and your swell friend making it?" she asked.

"Oh, him?" said Masie, patting her side curls. "He ain't in it any more. Say, Lu, what do you think that fellow wanted me to do?"

"Go on stage?" guessed Lulu, breathlessly.

"Nit. He's too cheap a guy for that. He wanted me to marry him and go down to Coney Island for a wedding tour!"

The Last Leaf

*After forty years Old Behrman finally painted his master-
piece—the strangest one you could ever imagine.*

In a little district west of Washington Square the streets
have run crazy and broken themselves into small strips called
"places." These "places" make strange angles and curves. One
street crosses itself a time or two. An artist once discovered
a valuable possibility in this street. Suppose a collector with a
bill for paints, paper, and canvas should, in traversing this
route, suddenly meet himself coming back, without a cent
having been paid on account!

So, to quaint old Greenwich Village[1] the art people soon
came prowling, hunting for north windows and eighteenth-
century gables and Dutch attics and low rents. Then they
imported some pewter mugs and a chafing dish or two from
Sixth Avenue, and became a "colony."

At the top of a squatty, three-story brick, Sue and Johnsy
had their studio. "Johnsy" was familiar for Joanna. One was
from Maine. The other from California. They had met at
the *table d'hôte* of an Eighth Street "Delmonico's," and
found their tastes so congenial that the joint studio resulted.

That was in May. In November a cold, unseen stranger,
whom the doctors called Pneumonia, stalked about the
colony, touching one here and there with his icy fingers.
Over on the east side this ravager strode boldly, smiting
his victims by scores, but his feet trod slowly through the
maze of the narrow and moss-grown "places."

Mr. Pneumonia was not what you would call a chivalric
old gentleman. A mite of a little woman with blood thinned

[1] Greenwich Village in New York: a very old section of the city
still noted as an artists' and writers' colony.

by California breezes was hardly fair game for the red-fisted, short-breathed old duffer. But Johnsy he smote. She lay, scarcely moving, on her painted iron bedstead, looking through the small Dutch window-panes at the blank side of the next brick house.

One morning the busy doctor invited Sue into the hallway with a shaggy gray eyebrow.

"She has one chance in—let us say, ten," he said, as he shook down the mercury in his thermometer. "And that chance is for her to want to live. This way people have of lining-up on the side of the undertaker makes the entire medical profession look silly. Your little lady has made up her mind that she's not going to get well. Has she anything on her mind?"

"She—she wanted to paint the Bay of Naples some day," said Sue.

"Paint?—bosh! Has she anything on her mind worth thinking about twice—a man, for instance?"

"A man?" said Sue, with a twang in her voice. "Is a man worth—but, no, doctor. There is nothing of the kind."

"Well, it is the weakness, then," said the doctor. "I will do all that science, so far as it may filter through my efforts, can accomplish. But whenever my patient begins to count the carriages in her funeral procession I subtract 50 percent from the curative power of medicines. If you will get her to ask one question about the new winter styles in cloak sleeves I will promise you a one-in-five chance for her, instead of one in ten."

After the doctor had gone Sue went into the workroom and cried a Japanese napkin to a pulp. Then she swaggered into Johnsy's room with her drawing board, whistling ragtime.

Johnsy lay, scarcely making a ripple under the bedclothes, with her face toward the window. Sue stopped whistling, thinking she was asleep.

She arranged her board and began a pen-and-ink drawing

to illustrate a magazine story. Young artists must pave their way to Art by drawing pictures for magazine stories that young authors write to pave their way to Literature.

As Sue was sketching a pair of elegant horseshow riding trousers and a monocle on the figure of the hero, an Idaho cowboy, she heard a low sound, several times repeated. She went quickly to the bedside.

Johnsy's eyes were open wide. She was looking out the window and counting—counting backward.

"Twelve," she said, and a litte later "eleven"; and then "ten" and "nine"; and then "eight" and "seven" almost together.

Sue looked carefully out of the window. What was there to count? There was only a bare, dreary yard to be seen, and the blank side of the brick house 20 feet away. An old, old ivy vine, gnarled and decayed at the roots, climbed half way up the brick wall. The cold breath of autumn had stricken its leaves from the vine until its skeleton branches clung, almost bare, to the crumbling bricks.

"What is it, dear?" asked Sue.

"Six," said Johnsy, in almost a whisper. "They're falling faster now. Three days ago there were almost a hundred. It made my head ache to count them. But now it's easy. There goes another one. There are only five left now."

"Five what, dear? Tell your Sudie."

"Leaves. On the ivy vine. When the last one falls I must go, too. I've known that for three days. Didn't the doctor tell you?"

"Oh, I never heard of such nonsense," complained Sue, with magnificent scorn. "What have old ivy leaves to do with your getting well? And you used to love that vine so, you naughty girl. Don't be a goosey. Why, the doctor told me this morning that your chances for getting well real soon were—let's see exactly what he said—he said the chances were ten to one! Why, that's almost as good a chance as we have in New York when we ride on the street cars or walk past a new building. Try to take some broth now, and let Sudie go back to her drawing, so she can sell the editor man with it, and buy port wine for her sick child, and pork chops for her greedy self."

"You needn't get any more wine," said Johnsy, keeping her eyes fixed out the window. "There goes another. No, I don't want any broth. That leaves just four. I want to see the last one fall before it gets dark. Then I'll go, too."

"Johnsy, dear," said Sue, bending over her, "will you promise me to keep your eyes closed, and not look out the window until I am done working? I must hand those drawings in by tomorrow. I need the light, or I would draw the shade down."

"Couldn't you draw in the other room?" asked Johnsy, coldly.

"I'd rather be here by you," said Sue. "Besides, I don't want you to keep looking at those silly ivy leaves."

"Tell me as soon as you have finished," said Johnsy, closing her eyes, and lying white and still as a fallen statue, "because I want to see the last one fall. I'm tired of waiting. I'm tired of thinking. I want to turn loose my hold on everything, and go sailing down, down, just like one of those poor, tired leaves."

"Try to sleep," said Sue. "I must call Behrman up to be my model for the old hermit miner. I'll not be gone a minute. Don't try to move 'til I come back."

Old Behrman was a painter who lived on the ground floor beneath them. He was past 60 and had a beard curling down from the head of a satyr with the body of an imp. Behrman was a failure in art. Forty years he had wielded the brush without getting near enough to touch the hem of his Mistress's robe. He had been always about to paint a masterpiece, but had never yet begun it. For several years he had painted nothing except now and then a daub in the line of commerce or advertising. He earned a little by serving as a model to those young artists in the colony who could not pay the price of a professional. He drank gin to excess, and still talked of his coming masterpiece. For the rest he was a fierce little old man, who scoffed terribly at softness in any one, and who regarded himself as especial mastiff-in-waiting to protect the two young artists in the studio above.

Sue found Behrman smelling strongly of juniper berries in his dimly lighted den below. In one corner was a blank canvas on an easel that had been waiting there for 25 years to receive the first line of the masterpiece. She told him of Johnsy's fancy, and how she feared she would, indeed, light and fragile as a leaf herself, float away, when her slight hold upon the world grew weaker.

Old Behrman, with his red eyes plainly streaming, shouted his contempt and derision for such idiotic imaginings.

"Vass!" he cried. "Is dere people in de world mit der foolishness to die because leafs dey drop off from a con-founded vine? I haf not heard of such a thing. No, I will not bose as a model for your fool hermit-dunderhead. Vy do you allow dot silly pusiness to come in der brain of her? Ach, dot poor leetle Miss Yohnsy."

"She is very ill and weak," said Sue, "and the fever has left her mind morbid and full of strange fancies. Very well, Mr. Behrman, if you do not care to pose for me, you needn't. But I think you are a horrid old—old flibbertigibbet."

"You are just like a woman!" yelled Behrman. "Who said I will not bose? Go on. I come mit you. For half an hour I haf peen trying to say dot I am ready to bose. Gott! Dis is not any blace in which one so goot as Miss Yohnsy shall lie sick. Some day I vill baint a masterpiece, and ve shall all go away. Gott! Yes."

Johnsy was sleeping when they went upstairs. Sue pulled the shade down to the window-sill, and motioned Behrman into the other room. In there they peered out the window fearfully at the ivy vine. Then they looked at each other for a moment without speaking. A persistent, cold rain was falling, mingled with snow. Behrman, in his old blue shirt, took his seat as the hermit miner on an upturned kettle for ι rock.

When Sue awoke from an hour's sleep the next morning she found Johnsy with dull, wide-open eyes staring at the drawn green shade.

"Pull it up. I want to see," she ordered in a whisper.

Wearily Sue obeyed.

But, lo! After the beating rain and fierce gusts of wind that had endured through the livelong night, there yet stood out against the brick wall one ivy leaf. It was the last on the vine. Still dark green near its stem, but with its edges tinted with the yellow of decay, it hung bravely from a branch some 20 feet above the ground.

"It is the last one," said Johnsy. "I thought it would surely fall during the night. I heard the wind. It will fall today, and I shall die at the same time."

"Dear, dear!" said Sue, leaning her worn face down to the pillow, "think of me, if you won't think of yourself. What would I do?"

But Johnsy did not answer. The lonesomest thing in all the world is a soul when it is making ready to go on its mysterious far journey. The fancy seemed to possess her more strongly as one by one the ties that bound her to friendship and to earth were loosed.

The day wore away, and even through the twilight they could see the lone ivy leaf clinging to its stem against the wall. And then, with the coming of the night the north wind was again loosed, while the rain still beat against the windows and pattered down from the low Dutch eaves.

When it was light enough Johnsy, the merciless, commanded that the shade be raised.

The ivy leaf was still there.

Johnsy lay for a long time looking at it. And then she called to Sue, who was stirring her chicken broth over the gas stove.

"I've been a bad girl, Sudie," said Johnsy. "Something

has made that last leaf stay there to show me how wicked I was. It is a sin to want to die. You may bring me a little broth now, and some milk with a little port in it, and—no. Bring me a hand-mirror first, and then pack some pillows about me, and I will sit up and watch you cook."

An hour later she said:

"Sudie, some day I hope to paint the Bay of Naples."

The doctor came in the afternoon, and Sue had an excuse to go into the hallway as he left.

"Even chances," said the doctor, taking Sue's thin, shaking hand in his. "With good nursing you'll win. And now I must see another case I have downstairs. Behrman, his name is— some kind of an artist, I believe. Pneumonia, too. He is an old, weak man, and the attack is acute. There is no hope for him. But he goes to the hospital today to be made more comfortable."

The next day the doctor said to Sue: "She's out of danger. You've won. Nutrition and care now—that's all."

And that afternoon Sue came to the bed where Johnsy lay, contentedly knitting a very blue and very useless woolen shoulder scarf, and put one arm around her, pillows and all.

"I have something to tell you, white mouse," she said. "Mr. Behrman died of pneumonia today in the hospital. He was ill only two days. The janitor found him on the morning of the first day in his room downstairs helpless with pain. His shoes and clothing were wet through and icy cold. They couldn't imagine where he had been on such a dreadful night. And then they found a lantern, still lighted, and a ladder that had been dragged from its place, and some scattered brushes, and a palette with green and yellow colors mixed on it, and— look out the window, dear, at the last ivy leaf on the wall. Didn't you wonder why it never fluttered or moved when the wind blew? Ah, darling, it's Behrman's masterpiece—he painted it there the night that the last leaf fell."

While the Auto Waits

*The girl on the park bench tried hard to play a part, but what
a big mistake she made when she described the auto waiting
for her!*

Promptly at the beginning of twilight, came again to
that quiet corner of that quiet, small park the girl in gray.
She sat upon a bench and read a book, for there was yet to
come a half hour in which print could be accomplished.

To repeat: Her dress was gray and plain. A large-meshed
veil imprisoned her turban hat and a face that shone through
it with a calm and unconscious beauty. She had come there
at the same hour on the day previous, and on the day before
that; and there was one who knew it.

The young man who knew it hovered near. His piety was
rewarded, for, in turning a page, her book slipped from
her fingers and bounded from the bench a full yard away.

The young man pounced upon it, returning it to its owner
with that air that seems to flourish in parks and public
places—a compound of gallantry and hope, tempered with
respect for the policeman on the beat. In a pleasant voice,
he risked a remark upon the weather—that introductory topic
responsible for so much of the world's unhappiness—and
stood poised for a moment, awaiting his fate.

The girl looked him over leisurely; at his ordinary, neat
dress and his features distinguished by nothing particular in
the way of expression.

"You may sit down, if you like," she said, in a full, delib-
erate contralto. "Really, I would like to have you do so.

The light is too bad for reading. I would prefer to talk."

The vassal of Luck slid upon the seat by her side.

"Do you know," he said, speaking the formula with which park chairmen open their meetings, "that you are quite the stunningest girl I have seen in a long time? I had my eye on you yesterday. Didn't know somebody was bowled over by those pretty lamps of yours, did you, honeysuckle?"

"Whoever you are," said the girl, in icy tones, "you must remember that I am a lady. I will excuse the remark you have just made because the mistake was, doubtless, not an unnatural one—in your circle. I asked you to sit down. If the invitation must make me your honeysuckle, consider it withdrawn."

"I earnestly beg your pardon," pleaded the young man. His expression of satisfaction had changed to one of penitence and humility. "It was my fault, you know—I mean, there are girls in parks, you know—that is, of course, you don't know, but—"

"Abandon the subject, if you please. Of course I know. Now, tell me about these people passing and crowding, each way, along these paths. Where are they going? Why do they hurry so? Are they happy?"

The young man had promptly abandoned his air of coquetry. His cue was now for a waiting part; he could not guess the role he would be expected to play.

"It *is* interesting to watch them," he replied. "It is the wonderful drama of life. Some are going to supper and some to—er—other places. One wonders what their histories are."

"I do not," said the girl. "I am not so inquisitive. I come here to sit because here, only, can I be near the great, common, throbbing heart of humanity. My part in life is cast where its beats are never felt. Can you surmise why I spoke to you, Mr.—?"

"Parkenstacker," supplied the young man. Then he looked eager and hopeful.

"No,"said the girl, holding up a slender finger, and smiling slightly. "You would recognize it immediately. It is impossible to keep one's name out of print. Or even one's portrait. This veil and this hat of my maid furnish me with an incog[1]. You should have seen the chauffeur stare at it when he thought I did not see. Candidly, there are five or six names that belong in the holy of holies, and mine, by the accident of birth, is one of them. I spoke to you, Mr. Stackenpot—"

"Parkenstacker," corrected the young man, modestly.

"—Mr. Parkenstacker, because I wanted to talk, for once, with a natural man—one unspoiled by the gloss of wealth and supposed social superiority. Oh! you do not know how weary I am of it—money, money, money! And of the men who surround me, dancing like little puppets all cut by the same pattern. I am sick of pleasure, of jewels, of travel, of society, of luxuries of all kinds."

"I always had an idea," ventured the young man, hesitatingly, "that money must be a pretty good thing."

"A competence is to be desired. But when you have so many millions that—!" She concluded the sentence with a gesture of despair. "It is the monotony of it," she continued, "that palls. Drives, dinners, theaters, balls, suppers, with the gilding of too much wealth over it all. Sometimes the very tinkle of the ice in my champagne glass nearly drives me mad."

Mr. Parkenstacker looked interested.

"I have always liked," he said, "to read and hear about the ways of wealthy and fashionable folks. I suppose I am a bit of a snob. But I like to have my information accurate. Now, I had formed the opinion that champagne is cooled in the bottle and not by placing ice in the glass."

The girl gave a musical laugh of genuine amusement.

"You should know," she explained, in an indulgent tone, "that we of the non-useful class depend for our amusement upon departure from precedent. Just now it is a fad to put ice in champagne. The idea was originated by a visiting Prince of Tartary while dining at the Waldorf. It will soon give way

[1] Incog: short for *incognito,* having an alias, a false name to be used.

to some other whim. Just as at a dinner party this week on Madison Avenue a green kid glove was laid by the plate of each guest to be put on and used while eating olives."

"I see," admitted the young man, humbly. "These special diversions of the inner circle do not become familiar to the common public."

"Sometimes," continued the girl, acknowledging his confession of error by a slight bow, "I have thought that if I ever should love a man it would be one of lowly station. One who is a worker and not a drone. But, doubtless, the claims of wealth will prove stronger than my inclination. Just now I am besieged by two. One is a Grand Duke of a German principality. I think he has, or has had, a wife, somewhere, driven mad by his drinking and cruelty. The other is an English Marquis. What is it that impels me to tell you these things, Mr. Packenstacker?"

"Parkenstacker," breathed the young man. "Indeed, you cannot know how much I appreciate your confidences."

The girl looked at him with a calm, impersonal regard that befitted the difference in their stations.

"What is your line of business, Mr. Parkenstacker?" she asked.

"A very humble one. But I hope to rise in the world. Were you really in earnest when you said that you could love a man of lowly position?"

"Indeed I was. But I said 'might.' There is the Grand Duke and the Marquis, you know. Yes. No calling could be too humble were the man what I would wish him to be."

"I work," declared Mr. Parkenstacker, "in a restaurant."

The girl shrank slightly.

"Not as a waiter?" she said, a little imploringly. "Labor is noble, but—personal attendance, you know—valets and—"

"I am not a waiter. I am cashier in"—on the street they faced that bounded the opposite side of the park was the brilliant electric sign "RESTAURANT"—"I am cashier in that restaurant you see there."

The girl consulted a tiny watch set in a bracelet of rich design upon her left wrist, and rose, hurriedly. She thrust her book into a glittering bag suspended from her waist, for which, however, the book was too large.

"Why are you not at work?" she asked.

"I am on the night turn," said the young man. "It is yet an hour before my period begins. May I not hope to see you again?"

"I do not know. Perhaps—but the whim may not seize me again. I must go quickly now. There is a dinner, and a box at the play—and, oh! the same old round. Perhaps you noticed an automobile at the upper corner of the park as you came. One with a white body."

"And red running gear?" asked the young man, knitting his brows reflectively.

"Yes. I always come in that. Pierre waits for me there. He supposes me to be shopping in the department store across the square. Conceive of the bondage of the life wherein we must deceive even our chauffeurs. Good-night."

"But it is dark now," said Mr. Parkenstacker, "and the

159

park is full of rude men. May I not walk—?"

"If you have the slightest regard for my wishes," said the girl, firmly, "you will remain at this bench for ten minutes after I have left. I do not mean to accuse you, but you are probably aware that autos generally bear the monogram of their owner. Again, good-night."

Swift and stately she moved away through the dusk. The young man watched her graceful form as she reached the pavement at the park's edge, and turned up along it toward the corner where stood the automobile. Then he began to dodge and skim among the park trees and shrubbery in a course parallel to her route, keeping her well in sight.

When she reached the corner she turned her head to glance at the motor car, and then passed it, continuing on across the street. Sheltered behind a convenient standing cab, the young man followed her movements closely with his eyes. Passing down the sidewalk of the street opposite the park, she entered the restaurant with the blazing sign. The place was one of those frankly glaring establishments, all white paint and glass, where one may dine cheaply. The girl penetrated the restaurant to some retreat at its rear, whence she quickly emerged without her hat and veil.

The cashier's desk was well to the front. A red-haired girl on the stool climbed down, glancing pointedly at the clock as she did so. The girl in gray mounted in her place.

The young man thrust his hands into his pockets and walked slowly back along the sidewalk. At the corner his foot struck a small, paper-covered volume lying there, sending it sliding to the edge of the turf. By its picturesque cover he recognized it as the book the girl had been reading. He picked it up carelessly, and saw that its title was "New Arabian Nights," the author being of the name of Stevenson. He dropped it again upon the grass, and lounged for a minute. Then he stepped into the automobile, reclined upon the cushions, and said two words to the chauffeur:

"Club, Henri."

One Thousand Dollars

What would you do with your thousand dollars; Gillian didn't even have to think twice about his.

"One thousand dollars," repeated Lawyer Tolman, solemnly and severely, "and here is the money."

Young Gillian gave a decidedly amused laugh as he fingered the thin package of new fifty-dollar notes.

"It's such a confoundedly awkward amount,"he explained, genially, to the lawyer. "If it had been ten thousand a fellow might wind up with a lot of fireworks and do himself credit. Even fifty dollars would have been less trouble."

"You heard the reading of your uncle's will," continued Lawyer Tolman, professionally dry in his tones. "I do not know if you paid much attention to its details. I must remind you of one. You are required to render to us an account of the manner of expenditure of this $1,000 as soon as you have disposed of it. The will states that. I trust that you will so far comply with the late Mr. Gillian's wishes."

"You may depend upon it," said the young man, politely, "in spite of the extra expense. I may have to hire a secretary. I was never good at accounts."

Gillian went to his club. There he hunted out one whom he called Old Bryson.

Old Bryson was calm and 40. He was in a corner reading a book, and when he saw Gillian approaching he sighed, laid down his book and took off his glasses.

"Old Bryson, wake up," said Gillian. "I've a funny story to tell you."

"I wish you would tell it to someone in the billiard room," said Old Bryson. "You know how I hate your stories."

"This is a better one than usual," said Gillian, rolling a cigarette; "and I'm glad to tell it to you. I've just come from my late uncle's firm of legal pirates. He leaves me an even thousand dollars. Now, what can a man possibly do with a thousand dollars?"

"I thought," said Old Bryson, showing as much interest as a bee shows in vinegar, "that the late Septimus Gillian was worth something like a half a million."

"He was," assented Gillian, joyously, "and that's where the joke comes in. He's left his whole cargo of doubloons to a microbe. That is, part of it goes to the man who invents a new bacillus and the rest to establish a hospital for doing away with it again. There are one or two trifling bequests on the side. The butler and the housekeeper get a seal ring and $10 each. His nephew gets $1,000."

"You've always had plenty of money to spend," observed Old Bryson.

"Tons," said Gillian. "Uncle was the fairy godmother as far as an allowance was concerned."

"Any other heirs?" asked Old Bryson.

"None." Gillian frowned at his cigarette and kicked the upholstered leather of a divan uneasily. "There is a Miss Hayden, a ward of my uncle, who lived in his house. She's a quiet thing—musical—the daughter of somebody who was unlucky enough to be his friend. I forgot to say that she was in on the seal ring and $10 joke, too. I wish I had been. Then I could have had two bottles of brut, tipped the waiter with the ring, and had the whole business off my hands. Don't be superior and insulting, Old Bryson—tell me what a fellow can do with a thousand dollars."

Old Bryson rubbed his glasses and smiled. And when Old Bryson smiled, Gillian knew that he intended to be more offensive than ever.

"A thousand dollars," he said, "means much or little. One

man may buy a happy home with it and laugh at Rockefeller. Another could send his wife south with it and save her life. A thousand dollars would buy pure milk for one hundred babies during June, July, and August and save 50 of their lives. You could count upon a half hour's diversion with it at faro in one of the fortified art galleries. It would furnish an education to an ambitious boy. I am told that a genuine Corot[1] was secured for that amount in an auction room yesterday. You could move to a New Hampshire town and live respectably two years on it. You could rent Madison Square Garden for one evening with it, and lecture your audience, if you should have one, on the precariousness of the profession of heir presumptive."

"People might like you, Old Bryson," said Gillian, almost unruffled, "if you wouldn't moralize. I asked you to tell me what I could do with a thousand dollars."

"You?" said Bryson, with a gentle laugh. "Why, Bobby Gillian, there's only one logical thing you could do. You can go buy Miss Lotta Lauriere a diamond pendant with the money, and then take yourself off to Idaho and inflict your presence upon a ranch. I advise a sheep ranch, as I have a particular dislike for sheep."

"Thanks," said Gillian, rising. "I thought I could depend upon you, Old Bryson. You've hit on the very scheme. I wanted to chuck the money in a lump, for I've got to turn in an account for it, and I hate itemizing."

Gillian phoned for a cab and said to the driver:

"The stage entrance of the Columbine Theatre."

Miss Lotta Lauriere was assisting nature with a powder puff, almost ready for her call at a crowded matinée, when her dresser mentioned the name of Mr. Gillian.

"Let it in," said Miss Lauriere. "Now, what is it, Bobby? I'm going on in two minutes."

[1] Corot: a noted French landscape painter.

163

"Rabbit-foot your right ear a little," suggested Gillian, critically. "That's better. It won't take two minutes for me. What do you say to a little thing in the pendant line? I can stand three ciphers with a figure one in front of 'em."

"Oh, just as your say," carolled Miss Lauriere. "My right glove, Adams. Say, Bobby, did you see that necklace Della Stacey had on the other night? Twenty-two hundred dollars it cost at Tiffany's. But, of course—pull my sash a little to the left, Adams."

"Miss Lauriere for the opening chorus!" cried the call boy without.

Gillian strolled out to where his cab was waiting.

"What would you do with a thousand dollars if you had it?" he asked the driver.

"Open a s'loon," said the cabby promptly and huskily. "I know a place I could take money in with both hands. It's a four-story brick on a corner. I've got it figured out. Second story—chop suey; third floor—manicures and foreign missions; fourth floor—poolroom. If you was thinking of putting up the cap—"

"Oh, no," said Gillian, "I merely asked from curiosity. I take you by the hour. Drive till I tell you to stop."

Eight blocks down Broadway Gillian poked up the trap with his cane and got out. A blind man sat upon a stool on the sidewalk selling pencils. Gillian went out and stood before him.

"Excuse me," he said, "but would you mind telling me what you would do if you had a thousand dollars?"

"You got out of that cab that just drove up, didn't you?" asked the blind man.

"I did," said Gillian.

"I guess you are all right," said the pencil dealer, "to ride in a cab by daylight. Take a look at that, if you like."

He drew a small book from his coat pocket and held it out. Gillian opened it and saw that it was a bank deposit book. It showed a balance of $1,785 to the blind man's credit.

Gillian returned the book and got into the cab.

"I forgot something," he said. "You may drive to the law offices of Tolman & Sharp."

Lawyer Tolman looked at him hostilely and inquiringly through his gold-rimmed glasses.

"I beg your pardon," said Gillian, cheerfully, "but may I ask you a question? It is not an impertinent one, I hope. Was Miss Hayden left anything by my uncle's will besides the ring and the $10?"

"Nothing," said Mr. Tolman.

"I thank you very much, sir," said Gillian, and out he went to his cab. He gave the driver the address of his late uncle's home.

Miss Hayden was writing letters in the library. She was small and slender and clothed in black. But you would have noticed her eyes. Gillian drifted in with his air of regarding the world as unimportant.

"I've just come from old Tolman's," he explained. "They've been going over the papers down there. They found a"— Gillian searched his memory for a legal term—"they found an amendment or a postscript or something to the will. It seemed that the old boy loosened up a little on second thoughts and willed you a thousand dollars. I was driving up this way and Tolman asked me to bring you the money. Here it is. You'd better count it to see if it's right." Gillian laid the money beside her hand on the desk.

Miss Hayden turned white. "Oh!" she said, and again "Oh!"

Gillian half turned and looked out of the window.

"I suppose, of course," he said, in a low voice, "that you know I love you."

"I am sorry," said Miss Hayden, taking up her money.

"There is no use?" asked Gillian, almost lightheartedly.

"I am sorry," she said again.

"May I write a note?" asked Gillian, with a smile. He seated himself at the big library table. She supplied him with paper and pen, and then went back to her desk.

Gillian made out his account of his expenditure of the thousand dollars in these words:

"Paid by the black sheep, Robert Gillian, $1,000 on account of the eternal happiness, owed by Heaven to the best and dearest woman on earth."

Gillian slipped his writing into an envelope, bowed and went his way.

His cab stopped again at the offices of Tolman & Sharp.

"I have expended the thousand dollars," he said, cheerily, to Tolman of the gold glasses, "and I have come to render account of it, as I agreed. There is quite a feeling of summer in the air—do you not think so, Mr. Tolman?" He tossed a white envelope on the lawyer's table. "You will find there a memorandum, sir, of the *modus operandi*[2] of the vanishing of the dollars."

Without touching the envelope, Mr. Tolman went to a door and called his partner, Sharp. Together they explored the caverns of an immense safe. Forth they dragged as trophy of their search a big envelope sealed with wax. This they forcibly invaded, and wagged their heads together over its contents. Then Tolman became spokesman.

"Mr. Gillian," he said, formally, "there was a codicil to your uncle's will. It was intrusted to us privately, with instructions that it be not opened until you had furnished us with a full account of your handling of the $1,000 bequest in the will. As you have fulfilled the conditions, my partner and I have read the codicil. I do not wish to encumber your understanding with its legal terms, but I will acquaint you with the spirit of it contents.

"In the event that your disposition of the $1,000 demonstrates that you possess any of the qualifications that deserve reward, much benefit will accrue to you. Mr. Sharp and I are named as the judges, and I assure you that we will do our duty strictly according to justice—with liberality. We are not at all unfavorably disposed toward you, Mr. Gillian.

[2] Modus operandi: the working method.

166

But let us return to the letter of the codicil. If your disposal of the money in question has been prudent, wise, or unselfish it is in our power to hand you over bonds to the value of $50,000, which have been placed in our hands for that purpose. But if—as our client, the late Mr. Gillian, explicitly provides—you have used this money as you have used money in the past—I quote the late Mr. Gillian—in throwing it away among evil companions—the $50,000 is to be paid to Miriam Hayden, ward of the late Mr. Gillian, without delay. Now, Mr. Gillian, Mr. Sharp and I will examine your account in regard to the $1,000. You submit it in writing, I believe. I hope you will repose confidence in our decision."

Mr. Tolman reached for the envelope. Gillian was a little the quicker in taking it up. He tore the account and its cover leisurely into strips and dropped them into his pocket.

"It's all right," he said smilingly. "There isn't a bit of need to bother you with this. I don't suppose you'd understand these itemized bets, anyway. I lost the thousand dollars on the races. Good-day to you, gentlemen."

Tolman & Sharp shook their heads mournfully at each other when Gillian left, for they heard him whistling gayly in the hallway as he waited for the elevator.

Reviewing Your Reading

"The Cop and the Anthem"

Finding the Main Idea

1. The author is mostly interested in telling how Soapy
(A) looks for a job (B) tries to become a policeman
(C) tries to get arrested (D) eats a free meal

Remembering Detail

2. How long did Soapy want to stay on Blackwells Island?
(A) Three weeks (B) Three months (C) Three years
(D) Three days

3. The first restaurant turned Soapy out because of his
(A) coat and hat (B) trousers and shoes (C) shirt
and necktie (D) scarf and gloves

4. In the second restaurant, Soapy had a dinner of
(A) beefsteak and flapjacks (B) roast duck (C) beef
stew (D) cheese and bread

5. When Soapy was arrested, he was standing in front of a
(A) park bench (B) restaurant (C) church (D) cigar
store

Drawing Conclusions

6. You can tell from the story that Soapy
(A) had not had a job for years (B) used to work in
Madison Square (C) goes on a cruise every winter
(D) went to Yale for four years

Using Your Reason

7. When the author says that Soapy "seemed doomed to
liberty," he means that Soapy could not
(A) stay in Madison Square (B) get into a restaurant
(C) get arrested (D) find a job

8. Soapy's main reason for wanting to eat at an expensive
restaurant was that he

(A) liked to spend money (B) wanted to have the best for nothing (C) knew the head waiter (D) wanted to show off his suit

Identifying the Mood
9. After five unsuccessful attempts to get arrested, Soapy felt

(A) relieved (B) angry (C) happy (D) lonely

Reading for Deeper Meaning
10. The story suggests that no matter how hard you try, you can't

(A) control fate (B) get arrested (C) find a good job (D) get a free meal

Thinking It Over
1. Soapy preferred to spend the cold winter in prison rather than in a charitable institution. He thought that charity, but not prison, was humiliating. How do you feel about Soapy's attitudes?
2. Which one of Soapy's attempts at getting arrested do you find most amusing? Why?
3. Just before his arrest, Soapy imagined a new future for himself. If he hadn't been arrested, do you think he would have begun making plans, or would he have given up? In other words, do you believe that Soapy could suddenly change all of his bad habits?

"The Skylight Room"

Finding the Main Idea
1. The author is mostly interested in telling how Miss Leeson

(A) meets "Billy Jackson" (B) becomes a doctor (C) meets a young playwright (D) becomes an astronomer

Remembering Detail
2. The rent for the skylight room was

(A) $8 (B) $12 (C) $2 (D) $3

3. How old was Mr. Hoover?
   (A) 45   (B) 25   (C) 48   (D) 30
4. Who showed the skylight room to Miss Leeson?
   (A) Mrs. Parker   (B) Anna Held   (C) Clara   (D) Miss Dorn
5. Which roomer knew about astronomy?
   (A) Mr. Evans   (B) Mr. Skidder   (C) Mr. Hoover
   (D) Miss Longnecker
6. What is the real name of the star Miss Leeson saw?
   (A) Cassiopeia   (B) Gamma   (C) Delorme   (D) Erebus

Drawing Conclusions
7. You can figure out that the reason the men liked Miss Leeson was that she
   (A) was a good typist   (B) liked astronomy   (C) wasn't stuck-up   (D) was a good actress

Using Your Reason
8. Which of the following is the most illogical part of the story?
   (A) That Mr. Skidder had not published any plays
   (B) That the gentlemen roomers preferred Miss Leeson
   (C) That Mr. Hoover asked Miss Leeson to marry him
   (D) That the doctor's name was William Jackson
9. When the author says that the doctor "let loose his tongue" on Mrs. Parker, he means that the doctor
   (A) started to cry   (B) spoke sharply to her   (C) said nothing to her   (D) said kind words to her

Identifying the Mood
10. Which of the following best describes Elsie Leeson?
    (A) Snobbish   (B) Sensible   (C) Light-hearted
    (D) Silly

Reading for Deeper Meaning
11. The story suggests that
    (A) kind-hearted people are rewarded   (B) most people are greedy   (C) people like Miss Leeson are foolish   (D) make-believe is a waste of time

1. Why do you think Mrs. Parker was scornful of people who came to look at her rooms?
2. Discuss the differences between Miss Leeson, Miss Longnecker, and Miss Dorn. Explain why the gentlemen boarders chose Miss Leeson as their favorite among the women boarders.

"Mammon and the Archer"

Finding the Main Idea

1. The story is mostly about how Anthony Rockwall
   (A) sells his soap business (B) helps his son enter high society (C) uses his money for his son's happiness (D) lends his son money for a ring
2. The name of Mr. Rockwall's soap is
   (A) Nesselrode (B) Mazuma (C) Eureka (D) Wallack's

Remembering Detail

3. Where was Miss Lantry supposed to meet her mother?
   (A) In the Bahamas (B) At the theater (C) In Europe (D) At Larchmont
4. Who gave Richard the gold ring?
   (A) His aunt (B) His mother (C) Miss Lantry (D) His father
5. How long was the cab stuck in the traffic jam?
   (A) 1 hour (B) 45 minutes (C) 20 minutes (D) 2 hours

Drawing Conclusions

6. You can tell from the story that Anthony Rockwall
   (A) spoke to Miss Lantry's family (B) used his money to help his son (C) disapproved of his son's use of money (D) disapproved of Miss Lantry

Using Your Reason

7. When the author writes "the great god Mazuma," he means

(A) love   (B) time   (C) money   (D) luck
8. Richard's main reason for taking the cab with Miss Lantry was to
(A) give her the ring   (B) tell her he loved her   (C) get her to the theater safely   (D) make plans to travel to Europe

Identifying the Mood
9. Which of the following best describes Richard Rockwall?
(A) Gentlemanly   (B) Pushy   (C) Snobbish   (D) Weak
10. Which of the following best describes Anthony Rockwall's feeling toward his son?
(A) Impatience   (B) Anger   (C) Shame
(D) Indifference

Thinking It Over
1. Describe how Anthony Rockwall and his neighbor, Mr. Suffolk-Jones, seem to feel about each other. Why do you think each man feels as he does?
2. In your own words, describe why Anthony Rockwall calls his son Richard a gentleman.
3. Anthony Rockwall says that money will buy anything, including love. In this story, it seems that money does, in fact, "buy love." Do you agree or disagree with Rockwall? Explain why.

"The Gift of the Magi"

Finding the Main Idea
1. The story is mostly about how Della and Jim
(A) get Christmas gifts for each other   (B) visit their parents for Christmas   (C) have plenty of money to buy Christmas gifts   (D) decide not to give each other Christmas gifts

Remembering Detail
2. What is Jim's middle name?
(A) Dillinger   (B) Blake   (C) Dillingham   (D) Billings
3. How much does Jim earn in a week?
(A) $21   (B) $20   (C) $30   (D) $25.87

4. Dellas's hair is
   (A) black (B) red (C) brown (D) blonde
5. How much money does Della have at the beginning of the story?
   (A) $1.87 (B) $8.17 (C) $20 (D) 87¢

Drawing Conclusions
6. You can figure out that Della
   (A) is bad at saving money (B) wishes she were rich
   (C) does not work (D) wants to be a hairdresser

Using Your Reason
7. Della's reason for visiting Madame Sofronie is to
   (A) buy a wig (B) ask for advice (C) borrow money
   (D) sell her hair
8. Jim looked at his watch on the sly because
   (A) he was afraid someone would steal it (B) it had an old leather strap (C) it didn't belong to him (D) Della didn't like it

Identifying the Mood
9. When Della counted the money she had saved for Jim's present, she felt
   (A) miserable (B) frightened (C) happy
   (D) courageous

Reading for Deeper Meaning
10. According to the story, the best gift of all is
    (A) money (B) possessions (C) food (D) love

Thinking It Over
1. In what ways does the author make clear to you the poverty of Della and Jim?
2. The author says this is "the uneventful story of two foolish children in a flat who most unwisely sacrificed for each other the greatest treasures of their house." Do you agree or disagree with him? Why? Why do you think the author makes this statement?
3. What do you think Della and Jim might have learned from their experience?

"Springtime à La Carte"

Finding the Main Idea
1. The author is mostly interested in telling how
   (A) Sarah became a typist (B) Walter and Sarah were reunited (C) spring came late to the city (D) Schulenberg arranged his menu

Remembering Detail
2. How many meals did Schulenberg send to Sarah each day?
   (A) One (B) Two (C) Three (D) Four
3. What could Sarah see out of her window?
   (A) A box factory (B) A farm (C) The restaurant (D) A garden
4. What couldn't Sarah eat one afternoon?
   (A) Eggs (B) Pork (C) Dandelions (D) Pudding
5. What book was Sarah reading when Walter arrived?
   (A) *Gerard and Denys* (B) *Heart of Fire* (C) *The Cloister and the Hearth* (D) *The Lion and the Tooth*

Drawing Conclusions
6. You can figure out that the reason Walter hadn't written for two weeks was that he
   (A) was going to New York (B) was busy on the farm (C) was waiting for Sarah's letter (D) had lost Sarah's address

Using Your Reason
7. When the author writes about the "Lady in Green," he means
   (A) Sarah (B) Juliet (C) Springtime (D) Fate

Identifying the Mood
8. How did Sarah feel when she saw dandelions on the bill of fare?
   (A) Sorrowful (B) Disgusted (C) Astonished (D) Confused
9. How did Walter feel when he read the bill of fare in the restaurant?
   (A) Angry (B) Pleased (C) Excited (D) Indifferent

Reading for Deeper Meaning

10. Which of the following best describes Sarah's relationship with Walter?
    (A) Strained   (B) Romantic   (C) One-sided
    (D) Hopeless

11. Which of the following virtues is most rewarded in this story?
    (A) Kindness   (B) Bravery   (C) Reverence
    (D) Patience

Thinking It Over

1. The season of spring is an important theme in this story. Tell about the different things that springtime means in the story.

2. Is there anything in the description of Sarah's two-week stay at Sunnybrook Farm to suggest that Walter might not keep his promise? Why do you think Sarah began to doubt that Walter would arrive? Do you think she didn't show enough faith in Walter?

3. Describe the author's tone—his attitude toward his subject. Is the tone generally light-hearted, or serious? In what ways does the tone create an impression about the outcome of the story?

"The Romance of a Busy Broker"

Finding the Main Idea

1. The author is mostly interested in telling how Harvey Maxwell
   (A) finds success   (B) hires a new stenographer
   (C) makes an embarrassing mistake   (D) fires his clerk

Remembering Detail

2. How long had the stenographer worked for Maxwell?
   (A) Two years   (B) One year   (C) Two months
   (D) One month

3. In which season does the story take place?
   (A) Winter   (B) Spring   (C) Summer   (D) Fall

176

4. The story says that the business world has no room in it for the world of
   (A) sports (B) theater (C) nature (D) music
5. What kind of odor came in through Maxwell's window?
   (A) Roasted peanuts (B) Lilac (C) Roses (D) Fresh coffee

Drawing Conclusions
6. You can figure out from the story that Pitcher was usually very
   (A) reserved (B) inconsiderate (C) nosy (D) lazy

Using Your Reason
7. Miss Leslie's purpose in coming to work that day was to
   (A) interview job applicants (B) speak to Pitcher
   (C) fill in until a new stenographer was hired (D) see what her husband did at work
8. Which of the following is the most illogical part of the story?
   (A) That Miss Leslie would work the day after her wedding (B) That Pitcher would not have known about the wedding (C) That Maxwell would forget about his own marriage (D) That Miss Leslie would not be angry with Maxwell

Identifying the Mood
9. What was Miss Leslie's reaction to Maxwell's second proposal of marriage?
   (A) Amazement (B) Horror (C) Indifference
   (D) Amusement
10. Which of the following best describes Harvey Maxwell?
    (A) Casual (B) Lazy (C) Frantic (D) Dreamy
11. Which of the following best describes Miss Leslie's attitude toward Maxwell?
    (A) Patient (B) Disgusted (C) Self-sacrificing
    (D) Hopeless

Reading for Deeper Meaning
12. The story suggests that too much hard work can make you

(A) lose weight (B) lose your job (C) absent-minded
(D) lonely

Thinking it Over

1. Compare the different personalities of Harvey Maxwell and Miss Leslie. Do you think Miss Leslie is a good wife for Maxwell? Why or why not?
2. What kind of person is Pitcher? How does he fit into the story?
3. Describe the world of brokers and the Stock Exchange. Why does the author say that there was no room in the world of finance for the "human world or the world of nature"?
4. Can you think of any other ways that Miss Leslie might have reacted to Harvey Maxwell's forgetfulness? Describe them. Do you find her actual response believable under the circumstances?

"The Ransom of Red Chief"

Finding the Main Idea

1. The story is mostly about how two kidnappers
    (A) receive two thousand dollars (B) are arrested
    (C) end up paying a ransom (D) hide out with an Indian chief

Remembering Detail

2. The two men planned to hide out in a
    (A) tree (B) barn (C) cave (D) buggy
3. What is the narrator's name?
    (A) Sam (B) Hank (C) Ben (D) Ed
4. How old was Red Chief?
    (A) Nine (B) Ten (C) Eight (D) Eleven
5. How much did the kidnappers have to pay to return Red Chief?
    (A) $250 (B) $100 (C) $2.50 (D) $50

Drawing Conclusions

6. You can tell from the story that the kidnappers
    (A) were ready to plan a second kidnapping (B) made

178

a lot of money as kidnappers (C) were generally involved in dishonest schemes (D) would never do anything dishonest again

Using Your Reason
7. The kidnappers' main reason for choosing Johnny Dorset was that his father was
(A) an old enemy (B) very rich (C) a fool
(D) a bad father

Identifying the Mood
8. How did the kidnappers feel the morning after the kidnapping?
(A) Confident (B) Sorry (C) Afraid (D) Jolly
9. In the story, Mr. Dorset did not seem to care if his son
(A) ever returned (B) terrorized people (C) dropped out of school (D) became an Indian chief

Reading for Deeper Meaning
10. The story suggests that people who try to get something for nothing might get
(A) just what they always wanted (B) success and happiness (C) lasting friendship (D) more than they bargained for
11. The author would most agree with which of the following?
(A) The early bird catches the worm. (B) Crime doesn't pay. (C) Life is a bowl of cherries. (D) Easy come, easy go.

Thinking it Over
1. Do you think the story gives a picture of a typical nine-year-old boy, or does the author exaggerate? You may want to compare "Red Chief" with a nine-year-old child that you know.
2. Select and discuss passages in the story that you think are funny.
3. Do you find it believable that Bill and Sam are afraid of Johnny Dorset? Explain your answer.

4. What does Ebenezer Dorset's letter tell you about his attitude toward his son? What does he mean when he writes that he "couldn't be responsible" for his neighbors' actions?

"After Twenty Years"

Finding the Main Idea
1. The story is mostly about
(A) a policeman who becomes a criminal (B) a meeting between two old friends (C) how a city changes over the years (D) a missed appointment

Remembering Detail
2. The two friends were supposed to meet at
(A) 10:30 (B) 10:00 (C) 11:45 (D) 11:10
3. Which part of the United States did Bob travel to?
(A) The North (B) The South (C) The East (D) The West
4. Bob was waiting in front of a
(A) drugstore (B) five-and-ten (C) hardware store (D) restaurant
5. Which city was Bob wanted in?
(A) San Francisco (B) New York (C) Boston (D) Chicago

Drawing Conclusions
6. You can figure out that Jimmy recognized Bob when
(A) he saw the diamond scarfpin (B) Bob lit a cigar (C) he saw the diamond watch (D) he heard Bob's voice

Using Your Reason
7. Jimmy's reason for having a plain clothes man make the arrest was that Jimmy was
(A) afraid (B) unsure (C) upset (D) sick
8. Bob thought that the policeman walked up to him because the policeman
(A) was suspicious of him (B) needed a match (C) wanted to talk (D) wanted to know the time

Identifying the Mood
9. Which of the following best describes Silky Bob?

   (A) Shy (B) Depressed (C) Confident (D) Sincere
10. How did Bob act when he saw that the man who met him was not Jimmy Wells?

    (A) Hostile (B) Relieved (C) Afraid (D) Tired

Reading for Deeper Meaning
11. The story suggests that a main reason for living is to be

    (A) successful (B) hard-working (C) friendly

    (D) honest

Thinking it Over
1. Contrast the characters and the careers of Jimmy Wells and Silky Bob.
2. What are your feelings about Jimmy Wells's unwillingness to arrest his former friend? What would you have done in Wells's place?
3. Do you think Wells was right in putting justice ahead of friendship? Discuss your answer.
4. In what ways does the author create suspense in this story?

"The Furnished Room"

Finding the Main Idea
1. The young man is mainly interested in

   (A) renting an apartment (B) finding Eloise Vashner
   (C) living on the lower West Side (D) talking to Mrs. Purdy

Remembering Detail
2. How long had the third floor back room been vacant?

   (A) One week (B) Three weeks (C) One month
   (D) Two weeks
3. The housekeeper says that most of her lodgers have been

   (A) business people (B) gamblers (C) theater people
   (D) authors

4. The young man chose this apartment to rent because
(A) the rent was low (B) the location was good (C) he liked Mrs. Purdy (D) he was tired

5. The young man had been looking for Eloise Vashner for
(A) 6 months (B) 5 months (C) 11 months
(D) 2 months

6. What kind of people usually rented apartments in the red brick district on the lower West Side?
(A) Millionaires (B) Old men (C) Newlyweds
(D) Transients

7. The young man thinks Eloise Vashner lived in the furnished room because
(A) he smelled the odor of mignonette (B) she left behind her hairpins (C) she wrote her name on the mirror (D) he found her black satin bow

8. The furnished room was filled with all the following items EXCEPT
(A) a couch (B) picture frames (C) vases
(D) a bedstead

Drawing Conclusions

9. How do you know for sure that the girl who committed suicide was Eloise Vashner?
(A) The young man was convinced of it. (B) The odor of mignonette filled the furnished room. (C) Mrs. Purdy said she had a mole by her left eyebrow. (D) Her black satin bow was found in the bottom dresser drawer.

Using Your Reason

10. The housekeeper did not tell the young man that the last person who rented the furnished room committed suicide because she
(A) was afraid he wouldn't take the room (B) did not think he would be interested (C) thought the less said about it the better (D) did not want to upset the young man

11. The most illogical part of the story is that
(A) Eloise rented the furnished room (B) the young

man committed suicide (C) Mrs. Purdy lied to the young gentleman (D) so many people had lived in the furnished room

Identifying the Mood

12. Which of the following best describes the young man's mood?
    (A) Rested (B) Contented (C) Depressed
    (D) Thrilled

Reading for Deeper Meaning

13. Which of the following best describes the young man's feelings toward Miss Eloise Vashner?
    (A) Indifferent (B) Amused (C) Revengeful
    (D) Caring

Thinking It Over

1. Why do you think the young man decided to end his life? If he had found Eloise do you still think he would have committed suicide? What do you think he might have done?
2. Why do you think the author does not give the young man a name even though he is the main character in the story?

"A Retrieved Reformation"

Finding the Main Idea

1. This story is mostly about an ex-convict who
    (A) writes his memoirs (B) becomes a detective
    (C) opens a bank (D) becomes a hero

Remembering Detail

2. What was Jimmy Valentine's job in prison?
    (A) Cook (B) Shoemaker (C) Printer (D) Guard
3. How much money did Jimmy receive when he left prison?
    (A) $25 (B) $10 (C) $5 (D) $15
4. Where did Jimmy meet Annabel Adams?
    (A) Richmond (B) Elmore (C) Logansport
    (D) Springfield

Drawing Conclusions
5. You can figure out that in the end Ben Price thought that Jimmy would
(A) be honest (B) rob the Elmore Bank (C) make Annabel unhappy (D) go back to prison

Using Your Reason
6. When the author says that "Ralph D. Spencer passed away and Jimmy Valentine took his place," he means that
(A) Ralph Spencer died (B) Jimmy killed Ralph Spencer (C) Ralph Spencer left town (D) Jimmy acted like a burglar again
7. Jimmy's purpose in settling in Elmore was to
(A) be near Annabel Adams (B) plan more robberies (C) open a shoe-store (D) work in the bank

Identifying the Mood
8. How did Jimmy feel when he left prison?
(A) Depressed (B) Calm (C) Tired (D) Guilty

Reading for Deeper Meaning
9. Which of the following best describes the character of Ben Price?
(A) Reasonable (B) Unforgiving (C) Weak (D) Jolly
10. Which of the following qualities is most rewarded in this story?
(A) Diligence (B) Generosity (C) Honesty (D) Courtesy

Thinking It Over
1. What is your first impression of Jimmy Valentine?
2. What clues made Ben Price sure that the many bank robberies were the work of Jimmy Valentine?
3. Does the author make Jimmy's reformation believable? Discuss your answer, using examples from the story.
4. Describe the predicament Jimmy is in when Annabel asks him to do something about the locked safe.

5. Were you surprised by the ending of the story? What does it show about Ben Price?

"The Third Ingredient"

Finding the Main Idea
1. The author is mostly interested in telling how Hetty (A) finds a new job (B) brings two people together (C) rides a ferryboat (D) makes beef stew

Remembering Detail
2. Who was responsible for Hetty's losing her job? (A) The store manager (B) The interviewer (C) The buyer (D) Another salesgirl
3. How many years had Hetty worked in the Biggest Store? (A) One (B) Three (C) Four (D) Six
4. According to the author, Hetty's role in life was that of (A) shoulder (B) head (C) hands (D) muscles
5. Cecilia wanted to earn money as (A) a writer (B) an artist (C) a salesgirl (D) a model

Drawing Conclusions
6. You can tell that Hetty got the onion from the young man by (A) flattery (B) pleading (C) threats (D) persistence
7. The young man's reason for being in the Vallambrosa was to (A) visit his frind Jack (B) look for Cecilia (C) offer Hetty a job (D) look for an apartment

Using Your Reason
8. Which of the following is the most illogical part of the story? (A) That the young man would have no food at home (B) That the young man would be in the Vallambrosa that day (C) That Hetty would invite Cecilia to share her stew (D) That Hetty would lose her job

Identifying the Mood

9. Which of the following does NOT describe Cecilia's feelings as she jumped into the river?
   (A) Tiredness   (B) Hopelessness   (C) Cheerfulness
   (D) Unhappiness
10. Which of the following does NOT describe Hetty?
    (A) Carefree   (B) Serious   (C) Bold   (D) Sensible

Reading for Deeper Meaning

11. Hetty's attitude towards Cecilia and the young man was one of
    (A) a friend encouraging a romance   (B) an adult dealing with two children   (C) a bitter woman discouraging a foolish couple   (D) someone who needs food to make dinner

Thinking It Over

1. Compare the Vallambrosa Apartment House with the lodging house described in the story "The Skylight Room."
2. Give the reasons for Hetty's getting and losing her job at the Biggest Store. Why do you think the author describes both the interviewer and the buyer as "capable, cool-eyed, impersonal, young, bald-headed" men?
3. What does the author mean by describing Hetty as a "shoulder"?
4. Discuss how each ingredient of the stew tells something about the character of the person who donated it.

"The Clarion Call"

Finding the Main Idea

1. The story is mostly about how a detective
   (A) commits a crime   (B) repays a debt   (C) becomes a newspaper editor   (D) becomes a lawyer'

Remembering Detail

2. What did Johnny leave on Norcross's floor?

(A) A shaving mug (B) A peeled onion (C) A gun
(D) A gold pencil

3. How much money did Woods owe Kernan?
   (A) $1500 (B) $1000 (C) $500 (D) $5000

4. What was the name of the newspaper that Kernan
   telephoned?
   (A) *Morning News* (B) *Martian News* (C) *Morning
   Mars* (D) *Morning Star*

5. The reason Kernan gave for shooting Norcross was that
   (A) Norcross shot at him first (B) Norcross recognized
   him (C) Mrs. Norcross screamed (D) Norcross was an
   old enemy

Drawing Conclusions

6. You can figure out from the story that Barney Woods
   (A) wanted to help Kernan escape (B) admired
   Kernan's boldness (C) was sorry he owed Kernan
   money (D) wanted to see Kernan suffer

Using Your Reason

7. When the author writes of "mere fireflies of sound,"
   he means the cries of the
   (A) milkmen (B) newsboys (C) taxi drivers
   (D) police officers

8. Kernan's reason for calling the newspaper editor was to
   (A) order a copy of the paper (B) cancel an appointment (C) leave a message (D) boast about his crime

Identifying the Mood

9. Which of the following best describes Kernan's mood
   after the murder?
   (A) Regretful (B) Overconfident (C) Scared
   (D) Peaceful

Reading for Deeper Meaning

10. The author would agree most with which of the fol-
    lowing?
    (A) Pride goes before a fall. (B) The race is not always
    to the swift. (C) The early bird catches the worm.
    (D) A stitch in time saves nine.

Thinking It Over

1. Explain the meaning of the story's title. At what point did the meaning become clear to you?
2. Discuss the contrasting characters of Barney Woods and Johnny Kernan. What weakness in Kernan's character is his undoing?
3. What is the significance of the gold pencil and the button?
4. Discuss Woods's statement "I guess I'm a man first and a detective afterward."
5. Did you begin to feel at some point that the detective would get the best of the murderer? When and why?

"Schools and Schools"

Finding the Main Idea

1. The author is mostly interested in telling how an unsophisticated girl from the West
   (A) goes to college   (B) becomes a millionaire   (C) wins an artist's heart   (D) betrays a friend

Remembering Detail

2. Who was Nevada's father?
   (A) Jack Peyton   (B) Dick Warren   (C) Jerome Warren   (D) Mr. Fields
3. What did Gilbert's envelopes have in the upper left-hand corner?
   (A) A postage stamp   (B) A brush   (C) A palette   (D) A lilac
4. What did Nevada have in her valise?
   (A) Books   (B) Shoes   (C) Rocks   (D) Dishes

Drawing Conclusions

5. You can guess that the reason that Nevada asked Jerome and Barbara to read the letters from Gilbert aloud was that she was
   (A) impatient   (B) angry   (C) illiterate   (D) embarrassed

Using Your Reason

6. When the author refers to a "triangle," he is talking about
   (A) three people (B) a mathematics lesson (C) an artist's tool (D) a musical instrument

7. You can figure out that Barbara's reason for changing Gilbert's message was to
   (A) bring Nevada and Gilbert together (B) make Nevada appear foolish to Gilbert (C) have Nevada catch a bad cold (D) get Nevada into trouble with the police

Identifying the Mood

8. How did Barbara feel towards Nevada?
   (A) Affectionate (B) Indifferent (C) Inferior
   (D) Jealous

9. Which of the following best describes Nevada Warren?
   (A) Rude (B) Independent (C) Weak (D) Stingy

Reading for Deeper Meaning

10. According to the story, in order to get what you want you should
    (A) be yourself (B) act like you have money (C) read a lot (D) wait and see what happens

Thinking It Over

1. What did the author mean by saying that Barbara was the "hypotenuse" of the love triangle?
2. Compare the personalities of Barbara and Nevada. Were you surprised that Gilbert married Nevada, considering their different backgrounds? Explain your answer.
3. What hints of Nevada's inability to read or write are given in the story?
4. Why do you think Barbara tried to fool Nevada about the contents of Gilbert's note? What did she expect would happen as a result of her deception?

"Rus in Urbe"

Finding the Main Idea
1. The author is mostly interested in telling how Robert Vandiver
(A) becomes a successful playwright (B) wins the woman he loves (C) loses the woman he loves
(D) runs a summer camp

Remembering Detail
2. Which of the following did North NOT have in his camp?
(A) A butler (B) Plumbing (C) Ducks (D) A telephone
3. What restaurant did Vandiver go to in New York?
(A) Maurice's (B) Murray's (C) Pierre's (D) Jean's

Drawing Conclusions
4. You can tell that North hurts his friend Bobby by
(A) trying to win Annie for himself (B) reminding Bobby that he is not rich (C) not inviting Bobby to his summer camp (D) making fun of Bobby's plays

Using Your Reason
5. By "the favorites of Fortune," the author means
(A) children (B) swans (C) rich people (D) gamblers
6. Vandiver's purpose in staying in the city that summer was to
(A) write plays (B) go to the theatre (C) be near an actress (D) look for a new job

Identifying the Mood
7. Which of the following best describes Vandiver's feelings when he first saw North?
(A) Envy (B) Joy (C) Anger (D) Indifference
8. Which of the following best describes Annie?
(A) Kind (B) Ambitious (C) Selfish (D) Loud

190

1. Vandiver's description of North's summer camp is meant to be humorous. Give as many details as you can that strike you as funny, and tell why.
2. Contrast the personalities and lives of Bobby Vandiver and Spencer North. What was your early impression of Bobby's feelings toward his friend? What was the turning point in their friendship? Do you think the friendship will last?
3. Were you surprised that Miss Ashton chose to pick duck feathers with Bobby Vandiver even though she had a chance to marry his millionaire friend? Can you find any evidence in early descriptions of her that might have made her choice seem logical?

"Girl"

Finding the Main Idea

1. The story is mostly about how a broker
   (A) leaves his wife   (B) hires a new cook   (C) betrays a friend   (D) becomes a detective

Remembering Detail

2. Who is Héloise?
   (A) the present cook   (B) Hartley's wife   (C) Hartley's mother-in-law   (D) Vivienne's best friend
3. How old is Hartley?
   (A) 21   (B) 29   (C) 50   (D)39
4. How much did Hartley pay the detective?
   (A) $7   (B) $14   (C) $20   (D) $10
5. What color was Vivienne's hair?
   (A) Black   (B) Blond   (C) Brown   (D) Red

Drawing Conclusions

6. You can figure out from the story that good cooks are
   (A) easy to find   (B) hard to find   (C) expensive   (D) also beautiful

Using Your Reason

7. When Hartley tells Townsend "The kill is mine," he means he
(A) has killed Vivienne (B) will kill Townsend to get Vivienne for himself (C) is sure of getting Vivienne's consent (D) plans to kill his wife

8. Vivienne's reason for not contacting Hartley was that she
(A) was afraid of his wife (B) did not want to work in the suburbs (C) had a good job already (D) had accepted a job with Townsend

Identifying the Mood

9. How did Hartley deal with Townsend?
(A) Generously (B) Threateningly (C) Cruelly
(D) Politely

Reading for Deeper Meaning

10. According to the story, in order to get what you want you should
(A) take your time (B) be persistent (C) be gentle
(D) follow other people's advice

Thinking It Over

1. Were you "fooled" at the end of the story? Give some examples of how the author led you from one false idea to another.

2. Reread the author's description of Vivienne. Then discuss how the description is misleading in terms of Hartley's actual purpose in seeking out Vivienne.

3. What do you think of Hartley's threatening exchange with Rafford Townsend? How does it add to the "drama" of the story?

"The Whirligig of Life"

Finding the Main Idea
1. The story is mostly about how Ransie and Ariela
   (A) solve their problem   (B) cheat Justice Widdup
   (C) go their separate ways   (D) obtain great wealth

Remembering Detail
2. Ariela plans to live with her
   (A) sister   (B) brother   (C) grandparents   (D) aunt and uncle
3. Ariela needed alimony for
   (A) a dress   (B) a hat   (C) a pair of shoes   (D) an apron
4. Ariela offers to go home with Ransie to
   (A) cook dinner   (B) pack a suitcase   (C) wind the clock   (D) feed the dogs

Drawing Conclusions
5. You can figure out that the man who robbed Justice Widdup was
   (A) an escaped convict   (B) Ransie Bilbro   (C) Uncle Ziah   (D) brother Ed

Using Your Reason
6. Justice Widdup's purpose in telling Ransie he would be lonely was to
   (A) make him suffer   (B) start a conversation
   (C) make Ransie regret the divorce   (D) cheer him up

Identifying the Mood
7. How did Ransie and Ariela act after they got their divorce decrees?
   (A) Glad   (B) Angry   (C) Scared   (D) Uncertain
8. Which of the following best describes Justice Widdup?
   (A) Soft-hearted   (B) Shrewd   (C) Cruel   (D) Timid

Reading for Deeper Meaning
9. Which of the following best describes the Bilbros' marriage?
   (A) Changeable   (B) Harmonious   (C) Tragic   (D) Dull

10. The story suggests that a main object of living is to
(A) try to understand others (B) steal to get what you
need (C) make money (D) work hard

Thinking It Over
1. Explain why Ransie and Ariela want a divorce. Why do they change their minds about it? What "lesson of life" have they learned?
2. Trace the adventures of the five-dollar bill.
3. What kind of man is Benaja Widdup? Do you approve of his way of dealing with Ransie and Ariela? To what extent do they owe their reconciliation to the Justice?
4. Do you find the scene in which Ransie robs Justice Widdup of the five dollars amusing, or sad? Explain.

"A Lickpenny Lover"

Finding the Main Idea
1. The story is mostly about how a man and a woman
(A) become engaged (B) have an argument
(C) become enemies (D) get to know each other

Remembering Detail
2. Which of the following does *not* describe Irving Carter?
(A) Millionaire (B) Painter (C) Musician (D) Poet
3. At first, Carter felt awkward about speaking to Masie because
(A) it was a new situation (B) Bill was watching
(C) his mother was with him (D) Masie was helping customers
4. Which of the following best describes Masie's home?
(A) Depressing (B) Crowded (C) Quiet (D) Regal

Drawing Conclusions
5. You can figure out from the story that Carter doesn't usually
(A) buy gloves (B) meet shopgirls (C) go shopping with his mother (D) sit on park benches

194

6. When the author says that the park is Masie's "drawing room," he means that she
   (A) lives in the street (B) draws pictures in the park
   (C) has no other place to relax (D) loves being outdoors
7. Masie's reason for rejecting Carter was that she
   (A) thought he was cheap (B) didn't want to travel
   (C) didn't like his mother (D) didn't want to stop working

Identifying the Mood

8. How did Masie feel when Carter asked her to marry him?
   (A) Disappointed (B) Skeptical (C) Joyful
   (D) Angry
9. Which of the following best describes Masie's character?
   (A) Dreamy (B) Gentle (C) Timid (D) Practical

Thinking It Over

1. Why does Masie refuse to take Carter seriously? What does that refusal tell you about Masie's knowledge of people and of life?
2. Explain why Irving Carter is not "the perfect master" of the situation when he first encounters Masie.
3. Explain the misunderstanding that turns Masie against Carter. Do you feel that things turned out for the best? Is the end of the story funny, sad, or a combination of both? Why?

"The Last Leaf"

Finding the Main Idea

1. The author is mostly interested in telling how a young woman
   (A) becomes a successful artist (B) discovers a cure for pneumonia (C) recovers from an illness (D) goes to Europe

Remembering Detail

2. Sue and Johnsy met in
   (A) a restaurant (B) the Bay of Naples (C) Japan
   (D) California
3. What did Johnsy keep counting?
   (A) Sheep (B) Juniper berries (C) Days (D) Ivy
   leaves
4. Johnsy was sick with
   (A) flu (B) tuberculosis (C) pneumonia (D) love
5. What was Johnsy knitting at the end of the story?
   (A) A sweater (B) A vest (C) Mittens (D) A scarf

Drawing Conclusions

6. You can tell from the story that what Johnsy needed
   most was
   (A) the will to live (B) warmer clothing (C) more
   friends (D) more medicine

Using Your Reason

7. When the author speaks of "this way people have of
   lining-up on the side of the undertaker," he is referring
   to people who
   (A) want to work as undertakers (B) lose the desire to
   live (C) live near a funeral home (D) wait in line
   behind an undertaker
8. Sue and Johnsy's main reason for living in Greenwich
   Village was to
   (A) have Dutch windows (B) pay a low rent (C) live
   among artists (D) be near Delmonico's

Identifying the Mood

9. How did Johnsy feel when she saw that the last leaf was
   still there?
   (A) Depressed (B) Hopeful (C) Confused (D) Angry
10. Which of the following best describes the character of
    Sue?
    (A) Loyal (B) Scornful (C) Lazy (D) Greedy

Thinking It Over

1. Reread the description of "the stranger, Pneumonia"
   at the beginning of the story. Why, according to the

author, is Johnsy a victim of pneumonia? Extend your answer to include the doctor's ideas about why Johnsy was not recovering. What is your impression of Johnsy? Why do you think Sue did not also get sick?

2. Describe Sue's behavior toward Johnsy. Can you guess what their relationship is like at normal times, judging by their behavior during a crisis?

3. Do you find Behrman a sympathetic character? How does he feel toward the two roommates? What were your thoughts and feelings when you read the last line of the story? How do you think Johnsy felt when she learned how Behrman had finally painted his masterpiece?

"While the Auto Waits"

Finding the Main Idea

1. The author is mainly interested in telling how a young woman
(A) becomes bored with money   (B) falls in love
(C) behaves toward Mr. Parkenstacker   (D) overcomes her fears

Remembering Detail

2. What book was the young woman reading in the park?
(A) *Robinson Crusoe*   (B) *Gulliver's Travels*
(C) *Cinderella*   (D) *New Arabian Nights*

3. When Mr. Parkenstacker refers to the young woman's "lamps" he means her
(A) legs   (B) arms   (C) hands   (D) eyes

4. The young woman worked as
(A) a waitress   (B) a cashier   (C) an actress   (D) a nurse

5. Mr. Parkenstacker wanted the young woman to think he was a
(A) rich man   (B) cashier   (C) waiter   (D) valet

Drawing Conclusions

6. Which of the following best describes Mr. Parkenstacker?
(A) Gentlemanly   (B) Pushy   (C) Nosy   (D) Rude

7. Which of the following best describes the young woman?
   (A) Snobbish (B) Polite (C) Clever (D) Smart

Using Your Reason
8. You can figure out from the story that Mr. Parkenstacker would have liked the young woman more if she had
   (A) told him the truth about herself (B) let him kiss her (C) been older (D) asked him more questions
9. The real reason the young woman made up stories about herself was to
   (A) get a better job (B) make Mr. Parkenstacker go away (C) impress Mr. Parkenstacker (D) get her name in the newspaper
10. What mistake did the young woman make when she described the auto waiting for her?
    (A) She told Mr. Parkenstacker the car was parked nearby. (B) She said the car was white.
    (C) She forgot to say the car had red running gear.
    (D) She described Mr. Parkenstacker's car.

Identifying the Mood
11. How does the young woman probably feel toward Mr. Parkenstacker?
    (A) Superior (B) Hateful (C) Jealous (D) Protective
12. Which of the following might best describe Mr. Parkenstacker's feeling toward the young woman?
    (A) Indifferent (B) Disappointed (C) Thrilled
    (D) Annoyed

Reading for Deeper Meaning
13. The author would agree most with which of the following?
    (A) Don't count your chickens before they're hatched.
    (B) Honesty is the best policy. (C) A rolling stone gathers no moss. (D) A stitch in time saves nine.

198

1. At what point in the story did you begin to think the young woman was not telling the truth? What slip does she make and how does she cover up?
2. What do you think is the connection between the book the young woman is reading and her conversation with Mr. Parkenstacker?
3. Discuss the differences between Mr. Parkenstacker and the young woman.
4. Why do you think Mr. Parkenstacker said he was a cashier at the restaurant where the young woman worked? Why doesn't the author have the young woman show any surprise when she hears this?

"One Thousand Dollars"

Finding the Main Idea

1. Which title tells most about the story?
   (A) "The Serious Lawyer" (B) "The Reformed Nephew" (C) "The Blind Man" (D) "The Beautiful Actress"

Remembering Detail

2. How old was Old Bryson?
   (A) 65 (B) 70 (C) 55 (D) 40
3. When asked "what a fellow can do with a thousand dollars," Bryson did NOT suggest that Gillian buy
   (A) milk (B) a house (C) a painting (D) diamond cufflinks
4. How many people did Gillian ask about how they would spend a thousand dollars?
   (A) Three (B) Four (C) Five (D) Six

Drawing Conclusions

5. You can figure out from the story that Miss Hayden did not love Gillian because she
   (A) disapproved of his style of living (B) loved someone else (C) wanted to marry a millionaire (D) was devoted to music

Using Your Reason

6. Septimus Gillian's purpose in adding a codicil to his will was to make sure that
   (A) his nephew deserved the money (B) his ward received the money (C) Mr. Tolman did not make an error (D) his nephew would marry Miss Hayden

7. Which of the following is the most illogical part of the story?
   (A) That Miss Hayden would reject Bobby Gillian
   (B) That Gillian would ask the opinion of a blind man
   (C) That Gillian would give up his inheritance (D) That a blind man would have $1,785 in his bank account

Identifying the Mood

8. What was Miss Hayden's reaction when Gillian gave her the thousand dollars?
   (A) Gratitude (B) Astonishment (C) Sadness
   (D) Anger

9. Which of the following best describes the character of Bobby Gillian?
   (A) Impulsive (B) Greedy (C) Trustworthy (D) Self-righteous

Thinking It Over

1. Why do you think Miss Hayden refused to marry Gillian? What did she and the other people who knew him think of him?

2. Explain why Gillian tears up the memorandum. What does this action tell you about his true character?

3. What does Gillian mean by telling Old Bryson that people might like him if he "wouldn't moralize"? Reread Old Bryson's speech about what a thousand dollars can buy. Then analyze it for his "moralizing" by comparing the different ways he mentions for spending a thousand dollars.